# Teachable Moments

Sandra Miller takes you on her journey beginning in beautiful nature, the hard work of life on the farm, to exotic cities, countries, and cultures that expanded her horizons. In Teachable Moments, you'll meet the characters that made a positive difference in her ability to bring her dreams to reality. Her stories bring readers belly laughter, hoots, high fives, and occasional tears. She makes it easy for us to become her best cheerleaders and fans.

*Wishing you the best on your journey. Blessings, Sandra L. Miller 2020*

# Teachable Moments

## A Woman's Journey
## of Self-Discovery

*Sandra L. Miller*

ISBN: 978-1-6847-1817-7 (sc)
ISBN: 978-1-6847-1816-0 (e)

Library of Congress Control Number: 2020901733

Lulu Publishing Services rev. date: 02/14/2020

*"Enjoy the little things in life for one day you'll look back and realize they were the big things."* ~Kurt Vonnegut

Dedicated to my mother, Barbara M. Hauck,
who inspired me to see life beyond myself,
make a game out of work, keep the faith, and give back.
To my husband, family and friends,
who made my journey more meaningful.

# Contents

## Part Two
## School Years

## Part Three
## Taking Big Risks

## Part Seven
## Mother's Poetry

## Part Eight
## Mother's Favorite Recipes

## Part Nine
## Mountain Hideaway Recipes

# Introduction

*"Everybody is a genius. But if you judge a fish by its ability to climb a tree, it will live its whole life believing that it is stupid."*
~Author Unknown

Chickens don't know anything, right? They're just dumb birds that run around cackling and pecking and sometimes they lay an egg and sometimes they don't. Occasionally they end up on our dinner tables, right?

I was fortunate to be able to grow up on a farm, spending lots of time with animals, birds, and creatures of all kinds, and one of the best things I learned was that each one was infinitely capable of teaching me very important lessons.

Of course, work on a farm is never-ending, and my mother taught me not only to learn to enjoy my work, but to make it fun. So, I learned to combine my "outside" life, which included public schooling, with my family life working on the farm, and membership in the Mennonite faith. I absorbed the lessons of determination, discipline, diligence, creativity, individuality, and self-expression, and I learned how to make it fun.

That's how my chickens became educated, and that's how I did too. When I was very young I spent time collecting their eggs, counting diligently and reviewing my math problems at the same time. I learned to praise the chickens who did their homework laying beautiful eggs, and had patience with the ones who didn't lay eggs. I learned which ones would pay attention to me as I shared my homework with them, writing the names of the state capitals on the barn wall, as I fed them and collected their "homework" to bring to my mother in the kitchen. And I chastised the ones who took one look at me and wandered off to cackle with the rest of the class.

Come along with me and step into my adventures as I learned what it took to realize that I didn't have to be a tree-climbing fish, or a chicken who could recite the capitals. I could figure out and discover just how to be me.

*Note: The names of some of the people described in this book have been changed to protect their privacy.*

## PART ONE

# Growing Up Years

# Moving Day

*"The only way to make sense out of change is to plunge into it, move with it, and join the dance."* ~Alan Watts

When our family moved from our dairy farm in Lancaster County, Pennsylvania, to a vegetable farm located in York County, Pennsylvania, I was five years old. The move was a challenge for me, and I recall how sad I felt leaving the beloved place where I had been born. My birthplace was a farmhouse in the country near the town of Millport, bordering Lititz. We were a family of seven, which included my mother and father, four siblings, and me. We moved to a small town called Starview, 30 miles away. As for any recorded history of Starview, there is very little available.

If there was a prep session for our move, I missed it. We children were simply asked to help pack and get ready for the big move. I don't remember any discussion about why we were leaving our beautiful home, and I felt kind of in the dark about it. Being the youngest child, I tagged along and helped with little jobs. There was a lot of commotion and talk about what to do next. I wasn't afraid, but felt a little perplexed.

On moving day, many family members and old friends came together to help us. Their presence taught me at a very early age what it was like to be part of a team. We worked with grace and order like a colony of ants, going back and forth many times, as we loaded and unloaded the truck.

Dad and the men carried all the heavy things into the new house each time we arrived. Mother was very organized and had us children help carry items. She would explain where to place the things. The reward for helping was to be allowed to ride in the back of the truck, as long as we

1

promised to sit down and help to hold our belongings from flying out. It was summertime, and I loved the feeling of the wind on my face and the smell of wheat fields, flowers, and the fresh air. When we reached the Susquehanna River each trip, we would shout, "We're halfway there!" It truly was an adventure and I enjoyed the excitement but I kept wondering why we were leaving the only home I'd ever known.

Starview was unique in many ways. There was one main street with houses on each side and our new farmhouse was on a corner at the edge of town, bordering that road. It's unusual for a farm to be that close to town, but that's part of what made Starview unique. If you stayed on the main road past our place, going east, it would take you directly to the Susquehanna River. Many towns in the county of York, Pennsylvania, branched out from the city into rural communities, such as Manchester, Mt. Wolf, and Saginaw, which surrounded Starview. Even though I've not discovered how Starview formally got its name, I remember that when I was a child, we would often sleep out in our backyard under the stars and they seemed to shine brighter than anywhere else. I'd hazard a guess that starlight had something to do with our little town's name.

At first, I struggled with the noises in town—especially the traffic that went by on both sides of the house. Because of the stop sign on the corner by our house, it was normal to hear the cars stop and go. The sounds of traffic were quite a contrast to living in an extended lane with no traffic, as we had near Millport. Eventually, I adjusted and fell in love with living in Starview.

Our new farmhouse was painted white with beautiful green shutters. It had an attic, five bedrooms, a large kitchen, a large pantry, a study, a living room, and a dining room. We had a large garage near the four barns. In the barns we housed chickens, stored hay, and sheltered the cattle. There was also a smokehouse where ham was stored, a woodshed, and an outhouse. There was a washhouse where Mother had her washer to do laundry, not fun during the winter months without heat, though she never complained. Wash lines were hung from pole to pole between the woodshed and the house. We laughed so hard when we had to bring frozen clothing into the house during the winter to thaw. I can still see it lined up like people. During harsh winter days, mother hung the wash in the dining room near the stove to dry. The large yard was filled with lilac bushes and all kinds of trees, like the Japanese cherry, red maple, and beautiful pines. The lovely forest green hedge that bordered the property enhanced the look of the place.

After a long day of hard work, it was finally mealtime on moving day, and the women gathered like a bunch of cackling chickens, sharing stories, laughing, and enjoying their conversations. My aunt Maggie laughed the loudest and talked the most. She even made me laugh when she expressed her opinion without much of a filter, as she usually did. She had no conscience about declaring, "This frying pan looks like it is just plain worn out! I guess if you use it for every meal it will look pretty near tattered."

For moving day, Mother made food ahead of time, enough for an army. Just the aroma of her homemade potato soup, with the whiff of onion, carrot, and celery could have won first prize at the fair. She prepared a feast! Many of our relatives and old friends brought all kinds of salads and desserts to the new place. My favorites were always the mashed potatoes, homemade coleslaw, and the "seven-day pickles."

My aunts, uncles, and friends were fun-loving people and full of kindness. For us to live farther away from them would make a difference, but we told each other it wasn't that far and we could still visit. I learned there was a sense of community through moving. People showed they cared.

The men were less effusive, discussing business and sharing what it's like to relocate in quieter tones. I can still smell my Grandpa's cherry flavored cigar and see my uncles standing around. Every now and then there would be a burst of laughter from the men as well as the women. This would be our first meal at our new place. My mother cheerfully announced, "It's time to eat, let's gather around in a circle," and my dad said grace. Excited, we all got in line and filled our plates with food. We were blessed to have more than enough to eat. We ran out of chairs so we sat wherever we found a comfortable spot, even if it was on the floor.

The wrap-around porch at our new place provided the playground for us children, especially on rainy days. Our new house had a cellar where Mother would store all her canned fruits and vegetables like she did at Millport. The difference with this cellar was that it did not have a spring that ran through the ground floor, which was a great place to keep things cold. Mother was always proud of her canning accomplishments as she filled the shelves. She would modestly announce, "This year I canned 40 jars of peaches which is even more than I was able to do last year." Our new house had three floors above the cellar including the attic, and five bedrooms but no indoor bathroom until my teenage years, when my parents installed one. Oh, what a blessing that bathroom was! In most Pennsylvania farmhouses, there were no interior bathrooms or showers until the late 1950s.

It was a delight watching my mother and seeing how she made the new house feel like home. Her love and care for us glowed as she displayed her creations. I loved her curtains, handmade white lace doilies, and vases filled with ferns and fresh flowers. She was especially proud of her china and teacups friends had given her. I still can see her turning over a plate or dish and asking, "Do you know where this came from?" They were often from faraway Germany, Italy, or Poland, and I can see the twinkle in her eyes when she told us the answers. Was she happy moving away from her close friends? She never complained about the move or transition, and that set a powerful example for us as we all adjusted.

I loved exploring, running up and down the stairs, weaving in and out of the rooms, and enjoying the space. Later, when we were more settled in our new home, Mother would read to us before we went to bed. We were in three different bedrooms so she sat at the top of the stairs so we could all hear her, and read from the Bible or from books of classic poetry. After the move, Mother had two more children, making us a family of nine. She made it a priority to continue to read to us almost every night. I cherish those beautiful memories.

Having neighbors who lived across from us and being so close to the houses on each side of the main street certainly changed my world. Approximately thirty houses sat next to each other along each side of the road. All of the houses were white, with bright blue, green, or gray shutters. The front porches with rocking chairs and flowers complemented the coziness of each home.

From our front porch, one of my favorite places to play, I would sit and watch people. I could see the country store, one of my favorite places in the whole town. What a busy place it was, with people constantly coming and going. There was a beautiful, small United Methodist church with a cemetery across from our house. As I watched people come and go from this church, I wondered what kind of people they were.

On special holidays, I watched them visit the cemetery, putting flowers on the graves of their loved ones, which was foreign to me because our family's Mennonite religion didn't subscribe to that ritual. When we had lived in the country, we had not been in close range of any neighbors, so with all the activity around us at the new place, I felt like I was watching live TV. People became my entertainment as I watched them coming and going.

I still have vivid memories of the people I met in Starview. Little did they know how closely I observed their routines. I was a very curious child. I soon realized that I lived a sheltered life and by watching other people, I became aware that our family was very different. I had a strict father who tried his very best to enforce the many rules of the religious dogma of our family's faith, which did not allow for much freedom at all. I was taught out of strict discipline and intimidation, which created no small amount of fear, how to live my life. I learned many lessons and discovered that, when all is said and done, life is really all about how we deal with what comes our way.

Curiosity came naturally to me as a child, and the experiences that I created while tiptoeing around strict rules became my lifeline to living. Moving day was my first real lesson in adjusting to change and learning to observe people who were different. I was only five, but I remember the challenges of being uprooted and figuring out how to fit in to this new, and strange environment. Moving on created a new chapter in our lives.

# Faith Breaks My First Addiction

*"You will find a joy in overcoming obstacles."* -Helen Keller

For me, the craving and fixation of addiction started at birth and continued for five years. At first, of course, I didn't know I was doing anything wrong. My terrible addiction was sucking my thumb and no amount of persuasion was effective in helping me to stop. Later, I read that this is one of the first addictions a person can have, and it often begins before birth. When I was small, I engaged in this habit because it was soothing, comforting, and made me feel secure. I was the fifth child in our family, and Mother had her hands full living on a farm, so I had plenty of time to indulge myself without intervention.

My mother was a gentle and soft-spoken person. You could usually find her wearing her apron over her dress, smiling while she worked, no matter what she was doing. But by the time I was five years old, she became seriously concerned about my habit. She tried using different techniques on a weekly basis, to get me to stop. The pepper she put on my thumb tasted terrible even though it didn't stay on for very long. Taste some pepper all by itself and see if you crave more. It didn't take me long to go secretly wash it off. I found ways to avoid sucking my thumb for short periods of time, but the pepper certainly didn't cure the problem. Then Mother tried wrapping my thumb with band-aids, and they were a pain to wear. My habit was so intense that sometimes I sucked my thumb with the band-aid on, even though it was far more irritating than soothing. The whole ordeal became so frustrating that I often ended up crying about my problem.

Nothing seemed to work and one day she said, "Sandra, you don't want to be sucking your thumb when you go to school." She knew the kids would make fun of me, so she emphasized this over and over. And there was the health aspect, "Stop sucking your thumb, Sandra, you can damage your teeth." But I just smiled and kept on sucking. I had mixed feelings about her request to stop, and I tried, but I couldn't do it on my own.

Raising children takes time to figure out the things that come up, with a lot of creative trial and error, and patience. My mother certainly had those traits—especially patience, plus a deep and abiding faith in God.

Every night before I went to bed my mother would read a story, and we would say our prayers together. "Now I lay me down to sleep, I pray the Lord my soul to keep, If I should die before I wake, I pray the Lord my soul to take. God bless…" and we would name our family members and friends to bless each one.

One night after our usual prayer, Mother said, "Sandra, I think if you pray to Jesus and ask him to help you to stop sucking your thumb, he will help you." So, I thought very hard, and came up with a simple prayer that I hoped would work, "Dear Jesus, please help me to stop sucking my thumb. Amen."

I jumped in bed and put both hands under my pillow. My mother told me later that both hands were still tucked under my pillow when she checked on me before she went to bed. From that night on I never sucked my thumb again! I have learned over the years that prayers are not always answered instantly, but I believe that in this case, my simple prayer activated the faith I needed to cure my first addiction.

Looking back, I feel that one of the reasons it worked so well was because I experienced a faith that was full of the purity and trust of a child. I trusted my mother, and on an individual level, I truly believed Jesus would help me. I was a child who wanted to do what was right. At that time, I did not know what the full impact of prayer could be on me and this was the first time I turned to it for real help. To this day, it is a strong and sustaining part of my life. Whether or not my prayers are answered in the ways I might expect, I believe in a higher power, and the Divine is my guide and strength.

This struggle might seem trivial to some, but to me, the experience had lasting value. It was proof for me that where I placed trust and faith, along with right action, the result was clearly supported by the Divine. There is something special about having good memories and successes along the pathway of navigating life. With her gentle suggestion that I invite the help of Jesus, Mother planted a seed that night, about having faith and trust in the Divine, that continues to grow and sustain me to this day. With the help of the Divine, I seriously made an effort and aimed to change my habit, and as a result I sailed into first grade having successfully shaken off the attraction of my first addiction.

Hallelujah!

# The Country Store

*"What we remember from childhood we remember forever—permanent ghosts, stamped, inked, imprinted, eternally seen."* ~Cynthia Ozick

As a young girl growing up in a small town in the 1950s, the local country store was one of my favorite places.

Going to Mary's Country Store was even better than going to the park, which I also loved. I enjoyed observing the people who came and went. Most surprising to me was hearing someone cuss or swear, as I was not exposed to that kind of language at home. Seeing dear Mrs. Mills in her white socks with her black high heels always made me chuckle inside because I never saw women in my home or church wear that combination. The neighbor who was from Poland came to the store one day all excited, announcing in his strong accent, "I got a letter from one of my relatives who plans to come for a visit!" I enjoyed his accent but didn't understand his history of separation from his family, so the visit from a faraway relative seemed unusual to me. Granted, I was a sheltered child, so many things seemed uncommon to me. This was the start of learning about differences and how to accept or not accept them along the way.

I often overheard conversations about family problems and the weather. "It sure is a beautiful day to work in the garden," Marge said to Mary one day. "Yes, I have to get out there and pick the string beans that are ready," said Mary. "Oh, and did you hear that Valerie's baby has the whooping cough?" "Yes," said Mary, "it's going around again." Mary didn't carry many medicines in her store because in those days there were people who went door to door selling their products, like the Fuller Brush man who came to sell household products and the man who sold Watkins Products. Mother loved those brands, and I remember how she used Menthol Camphor Cough Suppressant Rub when we had whooping cough or a bad cold. She would rub it on our chest and throat and then put a cloth on top for the night. It had a strong smell, but the warmth of it was soothing. In those days when there was a serious medical situation our family doctor came to our house with his black case full of medicines. He was the kindest person, professional and caring. He was loved by everyone and well respected.

Mary's was a hub of activity in our little town for the women and children, as well as the men. People enjoyed coming, both to visit and to buy their groceries. Her bins of candy and dill pickles were a big hit.

This store was like no other in comparison with places like the huge Acme Grocery Store a few miles away, and what made it unique was that it was small, quaint, and personal. It was located in a lovely white house with green shutters and white pillars on the front porch, where two rocking chairs were placed. There was always a warm welcome for guests and customers.

Each time I stepped into the store, a bell would ring to alert Mary that a customer had arrived. She would promptly appear from her cozy kitchen, usually dressed in casual slacks and a cotton shirt. Sometimes if I went there during mealtime, she came out of her kitchen with her mouth full of food, smacking her lips, which sounded like someone stepping on molasses that had spilled on the kitchen floor. She always gave me a warm greeting and asked how I was doing. Mary reminded me of one of my aunts, friendly and caring, encouraging me in all ways, but most of all, to do my best in school.

The rows of dark brown wooden shelves held spices, canned food, cigars, and more. Delicious smells of chocolate candy flowed throughout the store. And the individual attention that Mary gave to each customer was her gift and blessing.

I loved when Mother asked me to go across the road to Mary's and buy a loaf of Holsom bread and a quart of Rutter's dairy milk. Stepping out of my home and into Mary's country store was like stepping into another world.

If Mary weren't in a hurry, she'd invite me to sit on her old brown bench, next to the large bins of candy and the dill pickles stored in a huge glass jar across from the freezer. There we would visit, and enjoy each other's company. I was always intrigued at how she ran the store. She, like a captain, kept everything ship-shape, all clean and organized and in its place.

Mother would always allow me to buy candy if I had extra money. Mary, of course, knew my favorite kind: the fantastic chocolate licorice, and it only cost a penny a piece. I often bought a handful of licorice pieces to share with my younger brother and sister.

When I finally returned home, my mother would ask, "What took you so long?" and I would say, "Mary and I got to talking." I think Mother knew how enchanting it was for me to go there, and how it helped to broaden my sheltered world. Mary was an excellent example of what a girl could do when she grew up. When I came home, I would often imagine myself being a storeowner and managing mine just as Mary managed hers.

Mary lived with her sister and two brothers in the same house that was connected to the store. I had never heard of siblings residing like this together in the same home. Each of these siblings was single and over 40 years old. My mother would tell us they were hard workers and played an essential role in their household and community. I agreed.

In those days, it was prevalent for people to play one or two instruments. Two members of this family were talented musicians. Mary played the piano, and her brother John played the violin. Every Sunday morning, I would see him walk to church carrying his violin to play in the service. I enjoyed watching how they lived. When it came to music, I felt we had a connection, something in common. My mother played the piano and sang. My oldest sister played the accordion, my next to oldest sister played the electric guitar, and my youngest sister played the piano.

Today we are bombarded with electronic devices. Fewer people play the piano and often are seen using a keyboard instead. The shocker for me was when, as an adult, I considered selling my mother's piano. No one seemed interested. It was hard to give it away! Even pianos are not as popular these days, because of electronic devices. Times have changed, and I'm thankful for the memories of my mother's music and my neighbor Mary and her brother's music.

When I went to Mary's store, I felt right at home. Many times on Sunday afternoons I asked my mother if I could go visit her. I had my reasons, which might fall under the auspices of tiptoeing around the rules of our home. I would make sure it was around four o'clock so that I could watch *I Love Lucy* or *Lassie* on TV. We didn't have a TV because it was against our religion, though my parents never said I could not watch it when I visited friends who had one. During those visits, I got to see the other side of the country store, where Mary and her siblings lived. It was very quaint and tidy. I loved their warm friendship and excellent hospitality.

What a treat it was to sit in Mary's living room, on a giant fluffy sofa where my feet could not reach the floor. Her sweet sister, Elizabeth, always sat in the beautiful over-stuffed chair nearby and was very friendly. I liked this room. It was cozy with lovely lace curtains and green blinds. The first time I saw this room, Mary's sister Elizabeth said, "I crocheted all these doilies on the chairs." I said, "You do beautiful work!" After our TV show was over, I would hang around just a few more minutes to see if Mary would offer me a dish of ice cream. Most times I was treated to my favorite flavor, the most delicious, raspberry ice cream I have ever tasted.

Mary's Country Store was the neatest place to go shopping as a child. When I entered, I felt all five senses enriched. Even when I knew it was time to go home, I hung around a little longer. Today I still hear the clanging of the cash register and smell the chocolate licorice. The influence of her kindness will always follow me.

Mary's encouragement and taking time to talk with me were real gifts. She made me feel valuable by the way she always listened. She showed me that one person can make a powerful difference, even just across the street at the quaint and cozy, tiny country store. I observed Mary as being a hard worker, yet she always made time to show kindness to her customers; she took the time to listen to their stories. I give her credit for being a great example in my life, both as a woman, and a person of integrity. I know she rubbed off on me when I became a teacher and later managed a Bed and Breakfast. Mary's was the voice that said, "Yes, you can do it!"

# I Spy

*"You can observe a lot by just watching."* ~Yogi Berra

Who were these people? I watched them from our wraparound porch almost every day, one of my favorite places to spend time when I was a preteen. Some would say, "She is spying with her little eyes on the neighbors again," but really, it was more my way of satisfying a natural curiosity than "spying." Regretfully, I never got to know these neighbors very well, but from observing and having a few visits with them, their ways made an impression on me. They were kind and loving people, respected in our community and I treasure my memories of them.

John and Myrna lived in the first house on the block beyond our farm. Walter and Irma lived in the house beside them in this row of homes along the main street. From what I could see, each house had a long sidewalk that led from the front to the outhouse and woodshed in the back. A long wash line was strung on poles from one end of the sidewalk to the other end. It was a tradition to see clothes hung on the wash lines every Monday morning throughout our neighborhood. Very few of the homes included a car garage, but along the walkway in front of them all, gardens and flowers galore created a rainbow of colors.

Their homes were adorned with brightly painted shutters against snow-white exteriors. Their front porches were supported with white pillars and were decked with rocking chairs where these people sat in the evenings. Most neighbors took great pride in their properties and yards. My mother always said, "It's that German influence; they were taught to appreciate what they had and to take good care of it." I'm sure that is also what inspired my mother to keep our home cozy and clean. It was in her genes, that German-Swiss tradition of neatness and orderliness.

Both Myrna and Irma usually wore cotton A-line dresses as I saw them come and go. This was a typical style during the 1950s. Some dresses were bought, but many were handmade with decorative rickrack trim around the sleeves and near the bottom of the dress. I was always fascinated with buttons, and Irma had many dresses with lots of buttons. These two women always made sure their everyday clothing was stylish, crisp, and clean.

Their hairstyles were similar, usually long, parted in the middle, combed back over their ears, and put up in a simple bun. They wore black, thick, high-heeled shoes and nylons, but sometimes Irma wore white socks with those heels and, to me, that looked humorous.

I did not see these neighbors mingle too often, but they appeared to get along. Everything seemed peaceful when I would sit and watch. Myrna's husband John often had me spellbound. He was a tall gentleman, soft-spoken, and helped Myrna whenever he could. She loved gardening and cooking, and he was usually right by her side. John was totally blind, and I was always amazed at how he managed. Myrna helped him, but I noticed that he was very independent. When John walked to the outhouse, I would see him put his hand on the wash line and follow it to his destination. I never saw him hold the traditional white stick with red paint at the end that helps to guide blind people, but he had ways to navigate his surroundings. I don't remember Myrna driving, but in this kind of community, it was not uncommon for relatives and neighbors to pitch in and help, and they often took John and Myrna out when needed to run errands.

Irma and Walter were two energetic people who seemed to be on the go most of the time. Like clockwork, every morning, I could see Walter with his black lunch box walk out to his barn where he kept his car. He would back out, close the large door, and take off.

Irma was a real homebody and loved every minute of it. She seemed to dance as she sprang from one task to another. I often saw her hanging wash, dog clothing, and blankets, and then take them down to be ironed after they were dry. She worked in her garden, making sure it was manicured. It was a joy to watch her with her two beloved dogs, Brownie and Rusty. Irma and Walter never had children, and I believe their dogs were as much a beloved part of their family as children would be. I grew up on a farm and was not allowed to bring pets into the house, but when I watched Irma care for their dogs, she talked with them as though they were her children.

One day, I stopped by her house to sell seeds for a fundraiser at school. When I stepped inside her cozy home, I was amazed to see two doll beds in the room off of the dining room, each neatly fixed with sheets, a cover, and a pillow. I commented on how much I liked them and she said, "Yes, they belong to Brownie and Rusty." I said, "They are fortunate to have you take care of them." She smiled and said, "I don't know what I would do without them!" I believed her because Brownie and Rusty were treated even better than some children I knew.

Irma's kitchen had an old-fashioned wood stove, with a long pipe connected to the wall. Nearby I could see dog sweaters on a small wash line. They looked like the doll clothing I used for dressing my dolls and kittens. I was so captivated with how she pranced around and talked with her dogs. "Now Brownie, you stay here while I go for some money to pay for the packs of seeds." I was scared to pet them because they didn't know me. But they were very calm and well behaved. I thought, *I sure wish I could bring our pets into the house.* I sat and took in everything, the pictures on the wall of Jesus, one of the American Presidents, and the large calendar with landscapes.

Irma had something cooking on the stove because it was close to dinnertime. She came rushing back into the room and said, "I sure hope my soup isn't burning, Walter will be home soon." Irma was very particular, reserved, kind, and kept her house spotless. I loved how sweetly she talked with her dogs. She seemed more interested in them than in me.

After I finished going from door to door, I went home and shared with my mother how many packs of seeds I had sold. I said, "I'm excited, and I hope to win the prize for the most sales." My mother said, "I hope too, that you will win. Here, I will buy a few more." I couldn't wait to get to school to see how everyone else had done. If you were asked to sell things as a part of the activities for school, you had to set out early because everyone else went through the neighborhood as well. The competition was intense! I came in second that year for the most sales and I think Mother's special purchase helped a lot.

"Oh Mother," I said one day, "Walter just pulled into his driveway at the barn." One of his rituals, when he got home, was to get out of his car, shut the barn door and go to the corner. He always looked around to make sure no one was watching, and then peed. "Yep, there he goes again, right outside in the open." Mother giggled, and trying to be serious, said, "Sandra, how many times do I have to remind you, it is not polite to watch him." And then we both laughed out loud. Maybe Walter was in a hurry to get to the dinner table. As he walked up to his front door, I often noticed Irma opening it to welcome him home. She might have known about his quirky behavior at the corner of the barn, but she never said a word about it to him, and we didn't either.

Sometimes I long to talk with those darling neighbors again, as the memories sing loudly. It might seem strange to some people how much time I spent observing the neighbors, but they were fascinating to watch. Without a TV, I learned to enjoy other kinds of shows. As I reflect on the town of Starview where I grew up, I realize it was a piece of heaven and a safe place to live.

I've heard it said that "fences make good neighbors" but none of us in the town of Starview had fences and we all got along. Everyone knew each other and we were all quick to help if needed. We were surrounded by many good and caring people which made our town a great place to live. I learned a great deal by observing others and was fortunate to have such wonderful neighbors.

# Hog Leaves

*"There is no greater disability in society, than the inability to see a person as more."* ~Robert M. Hensel

Norene's favorite song was "That Doggie in the Window," and she sang right on key. Several times a week, I would see her strolling up the road towards our place. As soon as we heard her voice, my sister and I would run into our chicken house and peek out the window from behind its cobwebbed curtains. We stood there intrigued by Norene's daily routine, but afraid to approach her or join in. My sister and I were afraid of her because at school, she was known as a bully. She was kicked out of school for fighting when she was fourteen. We never knew if she got into fights because others picked on her, or if she was the one who started the fights. Norene never returned to school.

In the little town where we lived, Norene's behavior was very different from when she was at school. In the neighborhood, she would dress up her dog in doll clothes, put him in a child's stroller, and walk up and down the road, singing at the top of her lungs, "How much is that doggie in the window?" She appeared to be happiest when she was with her dog, looking for hog leaves.

We had no understanding then, of the meaning of "special needs," but as she grew older, it became clear that Norene was not like other girls. She was a social misfit with the boys and girls when she was around her peers. By the time she turned sixteen, the age at which most daughters helped their mothers in the kitchen with cooking, and with other chores such as sewing and gardening, or babysitting small children on their own, Norene had developed a new, solitary routine. If she happened to see my sister or me, she would yell, "I'm collecting hog leaves for our pigs!" To find her "hog leaves," sometimes she would walk for hours along the ditch where the weeds grew, and pick armfuls of the biggest and fattest leaves. We just waved and smiled but never felt courageous enough to carry on a conversation with her because she was known to be rough around the edges. We were much younger than she was, so it felt safer to keep our distance.

One day after we'd seen her picking hog leaves for her pigs, I asked my mother, "What are hog leaves, and why don't we collect them for our animals like Norene does?" Mother said, "Why, I've never heard of them. I wonder if there's such a thing, or whether they're just big, leafy weeds that they feed to their pigs." We could see that collecting these goodies for her pigs was important to Norene. It was something simple that she could do to help with the chores, and that made her feel good.

Her unusual behavior made an impression on me. Oh, I dressed up our kittens in doll clothes and paraded along our sidewalks with them like Norene did with her dog. And I sang songs behind the trees in our yard, but I would not venture out beside the main road. I knew about gathering walnuts and picking pears, but collecting hog leaves wasn't something our family did. Our pigs ate corn and soybeans. Sometimes we would feed the pigs leftover scraps because of the belief, "waste not want not," meaning, if you are not wasteful then you will not be needy.

Norene taught me several valuable lessons. Though she never learned how to build relationships and socialize, she eventually discovered, at least, ways to live without hurting others. We were amazed at how her face glowed with pride as she helped with simple chores at home and sang like a lark while she worked, how she took loving care of her dog, and how she took such joy in collecting hog leaves for their pigs. Unfortunately, the kids at school never saw this side of her.

I learned by watching Norene that she was a special human being regardless of her differences, and it was important to treat her respectfully. My mother often reminded us not to make fun of others and that certainly applied to Norene. I learned what empathy meant at a young age and maybe that is why, as I grew older, I often cared so much about the "underdog."

Sometimes, many years later, I catch myself humming the song she sang, and I wonder what happened to her. I hope she is still singing.

# The Cemetery

*"Cemeteries are interesting. They're worth visiting and they're worth studying. If we take the time to listen to what the stories might tell us, we have a lot to learn."*
~Richard Veit

A neighbor came to my dad one day and asked, "Would you consider taking care of our church's cemetery?" My dad thought for a moment and said, "I'll see that it gets done." The United Methodist church's cemetery was across from our house. It had about 100 tombstones. I often watched people come and go as they visited the gravesites of their loved ones and placed flowers upon them and some even posted an American flag.

That night at the dinner table, my dad asked if I would be willing to mow the grass and trim around each stone, at least once a month, or when needed, and especially before holidays like Memorial Day and Labor Day. The man would pay us $100.00 each time, but I wasn't sure if I would get any of the money, because in those days we didn't get paid for doing chores. I didn't earn money until I was sixteen when I began babysitting. I was now fifteen and had plenty of tasks to do, but I thought it would be kind of fun, so I replied, "Sure I'll do it." I didn't imagine how hard it would be, I just said yes on a whim, and that's how I got the job.

The cemetery had a chain fence around it and included a small area where I could put the weeds and dead flowers. I found that taking care of the cemetery was fascinating, especially when I trimmed around the tombstones. Some of the stones were fancy and had sheep statues, a cross, or a beautiful angel placed on top of the stone. Some had no unique decorations at all. This place was new territory for me on many levels.

Decorative stones, flowers, and flags were not seen in most conservative Mennonite cemeteries.

Reading epitaphs in different cemeteries was always fascinating to me. "A friend to all," "A godly man who served the Lord all his days," "A life of beauty and service," and "A man greatly loved." In this cemetery I would sit and wonder what the person had really been like. Did they ever hear those kind words when they were living? Were they nice and loving people? Sometimes it took me a long time to get my trimming done because I got so engrossed in imagining the personal stories that these stark stones represented.

I wondered when the custom of putting flowers on gravesites began. I learned that, along with many different cultural traditions both ancient and contemporary, acclaimed historian Jay Winik proposed that the tradition began in America at the end of the Civil War. It started after a train had delivered Abraham Lincoln to his final resting place in Springfield, Illinois. Winik wrote: "Searching for some way to express their grief, countless Americans gravitated to bouquets of flowers: lilacs, roses, and orange blossoms, anything which was in bloom across the land. Thus was born a new tradition: laying flowers at a funeral." (Retrieved from https://www.neatorama.com/2016/05/30/Why-Are-Flowers-Placed-on-Graves/)

My first experience with death was with my grandparents. I was with each of them when they died of natural causes in their home. I was ten years old when my grandfather died and nine years later my grandmother died when I was nineteen. My aunt and mother were there and I remember the gentleness they showed. At times there was a heavy silence and soft crying and I took it all in, learning that this was part of life. I specifically remember when the undertaker came to take my grandfather to the funeral home after he died. In a few days we had a viewing and a service at the church where the whole congregation was invited along with outside friends and family. Afterwards, we all paraded to the gravesite where the pastor read more scriptures, and then the coffin was lowered into the ground. The event was very plain and simple without adornment flowers. Today it is different, and not unusual to see flowers in Mennonite cemeteries.

Our parents did not discuss politics, or certain military holidays like Memorial Day and Veterans Day, let alone explain flowers and flags in a cemetery. I pledged allegiance to the flag in school, but at home, we did not talk about it, so now, looking back, I know that I went through the motions along with my peers, not really understanding the meaning behind the traditions. At one point there was a question of whether or not I should pledge allegiance to the flag at school, as was our routine in the classroom. I'd guess that my parents decided in favor of social acceptance by my teachers and classmates, since they never told me not to. After all, I went to a public school.

We did learn about the presidents and heard the news and current events, but very little was ever discussed. It all came down to my parents' religious beliefs. Being pacifists and peacemakers, very little was mentioned about "the other side of peace," like joining the Army, Air Force, Marine, Navy, or Coast Guard, or commemorating military participation by putting flags on the tombstones of those who had served in a war. So, there I was, in the United Methodist cemetery, placing flags on particular monuments, and I didn't understand why. The only thing I knew was that our church was firmly against fighting in the war, or at any other time. The young people who were members of the church were encouraged to become conscientious objectors. If they chose this path they could do alternative civilian service, "on the grounds of freedom of thought, conscience, or religion."

We children certainly wondered why our family didn't do the same things as other people. Usually we were afraid to ask questions, because, while growing up, we were taught not to question authority, talk back, or give an opinion. For the most part, we were sheltered from the many differences outside our home. When I noticed something that looked unusual to me, I just kept my questions to myself, but that didn't stop my unending curiosity. My home life was even more strict than most I'm sure, at my father's insistence. Just like the Mennonite churches, some families were more conservative than others, and mine happened to be in the very conservative camp.

Members of the Mennonite church were pacifists. If a Mennonite signed up for the military, they were automatically considered an outcast by most of the church community. There was a lot of discussion among church leaders as to what parents should or should not allow their children to do.

I will never forget the day my brother, who was a few years older than I was, and felt strongly about working in service for our country, told my parents he was going to join the Air Force. That was like telling my parents, "I disagree with your beliefs and religion." It was like a slap in the face to them, but what I will always remember is how my mother handled the situation and still loved him unconditionally even though my father and the church leaders were in an uproar. My brother was now rejected by many church leaders, which I had difficulty understanding, while my mother, standing firm in her faith in God as well as in my brother, prayed for him. That example of Mother's unconditional love stayed with me forever. My brother was stationed in Iceland and never had to fight, but nonetheless, he served our country. I missed him very much when he was away but he was faithful with writing letters and Mother would read them to us through tears of joy and sadness. After he left, I was the oldest child at home with my two younger siblings.

Despite the way we were raised, my brother chose his own path, and I admired him for that. I tried to find my own way as well, but was too afraid to go against what I was taught until much later in my life. Isn't it ironic how some of the ways that religion is interpreted and expressed can feel harsh, especially when it is designed to foster peace? In our religion, if someone went against the principles of the church, it could cause a lot of discord. In some cases, we were expected to shun that person, and sometimes even renounce them. I never understood how that could be "Christlike."

The cemetery became symbolic for me. Out of respect, those United Methodist churchgoers buried their loved ones and kept their memories sacred. They placed a flag in front of the tombstones for soldiers who served our country. They placed flowers for their dead, as tokens of love, respect, and beauty.

Today I certainly view a cemetery differently than when I was a young girl. Trimming the grass around those tombstones gave me plenty of time to think about differences. The cemetery, flowers, and flags have meaning that I now understand, value, and respect.

# Mother's Imprints

*"My mother...she is beautiful, softened at the edges and tempered with a spine of steel. I want to grow old and be like her."* -Jodi Picoult

I was blessed with a good-natured and hard-working mother. She glowed with beauty inside and out and was the pillar in our family. She skipped to a rhythmic beat with her work routine. Besides preparing three meals a day, she washed on Mondays, ironed on Tuesdays, mended clothing, and sewed dresses, sometimes designing her own patterns. She worked in the garden on Wednesdays, and cleaned the house Thursdays. On Fridays and Saturdays, she made sure all the walks, porches, and vehicles were cleaned with the help of her seven children. She was steadfast in her faith, loved to laugh, and took time to connect with others. Her good qualities far outweighed her flaws.

My mother had a full plate of activities in life, and it appeared she enjoyed the balance with delight. She seemed to live life with confidence, knowing what she had to do to keep the wheels turning. But that doesn't mean those wheels never got stuck or went spinning. Her way to get back on track and move forward was to face her challenges. Having seven children indeed tested her strengths and weaknesses.

By the time we children started elementary school, we were old enough to join her work routines. All seven siblings learned what it meant to work hard. The reminder hung in the air straight from scripture, "If you don't work you don't eat." That was farm life, learning the value of working hard for what we wanted. Don't expect handouts, only hand-me-downs. Those were the days when life seemed much more straightforward than today, even though we had our share of challenges.

When anyone visited our home, my mother would welcome them graciously and often invited them for meals. Having Sunday guests for lunch was the norm, and Mother always wore her beautiful cotton floral apron while she prepared her mouthwatering dinners. The aroma streamed through the house, making everyone hungry, as she made her tender roast with carrots and onions, along with mashed potatoes and more vegetables. To top it off was a delicious pudding and chocolate cake. She was amazing!

During the 1950s, we often had strangers come to the door who asked for food. They were called "hobos," "tramps" or "gypsies," and Mother treated them with kindness and respect, as she did all of the friends and relatives who came to our table. I would clasp my mother's apron when a stranger came to the door, and watch and listen from behind the safety of her skirts. She would not allow me to go out on the porch to meet these people, and if she didn't know them, she rarely invited them inside. I was allowed to watch through the screen door. Mother would chat and kindly tell them she would be right back as she headed back to her kitchen. Wow, she would return with a heaping plate of homemade food "fit for a king," with plenty of meat, mashed potatoes, and vegetables. Mother would have a short, friendly conversation with them before they left, and always wished them well on their journeys.

Even though she had seven children, and worked almost nonstop, sometimes I would get a glimpse of her softer, feminine side. Each month, a dear neighbor came for a visit. Mrs. Miller, the Avon lady, who strolled through our small neighborhood selling her goods, would knock on the door and cheerfully say, "Avon Calling! How are you on this beautiful day, Barbara?" "Fine," my mother always said, "I am doing well." I loved watching Mother as she welcomed Mrs. Miller in, and offered her a seat. "Would you like a cup of tea? I just baked a cherry pie to top it off," my mother would cheerfully announce. "I certainly would love a cup of tea and to taste your pie," Mrs. Miller would reply. To this day, I cherish the aroma of mint tea and Mother's iced cold "meadow tea." We grew the meadow tea leaves near the garden and it was always a wonderful summer treat. I loved sitting at the table listening to their conversations, while they chatted like most women enjoy doing.

In a short time, Mrs. Miller would ask my mother if she would like to see the most recent Avon products. She handed her an Avon book to look at while she arranged a display of the rose smelling perfumes, cherry red lipsticks, lotions, and sparkly jewelry on the table. Mother did not wear jewelry, but she loved the perfumes and lotions. Lavender and Lily of the Valley were her favorite fragrances. Mother usually bought one or two decorative bottles of sweet-smelling goods as Mrs. Miller gathered her products and cheerfully announced, "Here are a few free samples, and I'll see you next month." Mother would smile and say she looked forward to seeing her again. I was like a little sponge taking it all in and could not wait for mother to give me one of the samples.

Mother's connection with the Avon lady was a luxury for her, since there was no end to the work that had to be done. Shopping was often taken care of by ordering from the thick Sears catalog, or we could drive several miles to the five and dime store. The convenience of having the Avon lady come to our house gave my mother a social connection and time to buy something special for herself. She was very thrifty, but understood the value of a little self-indulgence now and then.

As close as my own shadow, my mother's beautiful spirit follows me, and I smile within. "Avon Calling!" These days, I enjoy chatting with my Avon lady, and I love to buy the lavender lotion in memory of my mother. I will always remember Mother's giving spirit and her connection with others as her legacy.

# Our Children

### Barbara M. Hauck (Mother)

Dear Lord, these children you've given us
Are treasures that are placed in our trust.
So thankful for their health and sight
For features normal and mentally bright.

The first one lent was a little girl
Dolores we named her, she had many a curl.
Her eyes were bright blue, so they stayed
Her liking was music, the piano she played.

Then next was David, with blond hair and blue eyes
So close to his sister in age, in things to do.
The two had interests so much the same
Not often a friction in the choice of a game.

The third to come and add joy around our table
Was Yvonne who cooed and smiled soon as she was able.
She joined the two older ones as she grew up
In throwing a ball or in cuddling the pup.

Karl was number four, our home to bless
His hair was blond and eyes blue you can guess.
His smile was a winner of many a friend
He liked to sing little songs from beginning to end.

*Sandra L. Miller*

Sandra's coming was number five
She had thick black hair when she arrived.
She liked to play and run on the "wall"
I guess it made her think she was tall.

Delmar's arrival was in the month of May
With flowers in bloom and birds singing so gay.
His brothers and sisters had lots of fun
Helping him play, watching him run.

Then on August 4th another girl came
It was sunrise, so we chose Dawn for her name.
Thus, adding to seven children in all
All happy together from big to the small.

My prayer O Lord, and this my plea,
That they will live in the light of eternity.

# Girl, Boy, Girl, Boy

*"Siblings are the people we practice on, the people who teach us about fairness and cooperation and kindness and caring—quite often the hard way."* ~Pamela Dugdale

I can still hear the smile in her voice as my mother shared stories about my siblings. She would tell people. "Our seven children, all with blue eyes, came into this world one by one, uniquely lined up as girl, boy, girl, boy, all the way to our youngest girl." She was so proud, in her quiet way, of each child. After the first four children were born, my parents moved from where they lived on a farm in Lancaster County to the farm near Millport where I was born.

*Did Mother dream of having four children in a row, not knowing there would be three more on the way later?* I wondered. Having large families was common in those days, especially for those living on farms, and she seemed to go with the flow. I believe she enjoyed being a mother and worked hard at keeping our growing family together.

I learned as I got older that when there are seven children, with more than a decade separating some of them, they can feel like they had different parents when comparing childhood stories. When we shared our experiences about our childhoods, our stories differed a lot on how our parents parented. My oldest four siblings, Dolores, David, Yvonne, and Karl saw themselves as the "real farm children" in our family who did most of the chores. They had to walk the tightrope and stay in line, just as we did. They often declared "Sandra, we had to work much harder than you three little ones did." I would not argue with that because it was their story, but I'd hazard a guess that they might have missed the heavier parts of the younger siblings' farm work since they left home to get married around the time we headed into our strongest years.

My oldest sisters told me stories about the four of them walking to the one-room schoolhouse not far from the farm, carrying their little lunch boxes with them. Dolores was confident and independent as the oldest. She became the leader of the pack. She appeared to be on a mission as she helped with the chores and led the way. She remembers milking the cows, yes, by hand! Many people often say, as the oldest child, that they felt like they had to take charge and be the leader. Dolores fit that profile and did a great job.

She married right after high school and had five beautiful children. Later she started a sewing school in York County called the Dolores Sewing Academy. She was very successful and loved her work. When we were planning our wedding, I asked if she would make my wedding dress. It was simple but beautiful, and I wore it with pride. Dolores and I are ten years apart and I'm so glad that in our later years, we got to know each other much better than when I was growing up.

One day when I was young, she asked me if I'd like to join her on a bike ride, and of course, I said "Yes, me too!" So I clambered up behind her onto a narrow, little seat. My legs dangled on each side, and off we went, but we didn't get very far, because my left foot got caught in the spokes! I started screaming. She was born with my mother's calm, and she simply stopped and scooped me up, taking me into the house without any hysterics about all the blood. I'm certain today I would have been taken to the doctor, but when I was growing up, we were used to being much more independent about injuries. So Mother cleaned up and disinfected my wounds, and wrapped them in sterile bandages. She bandaged tightly to help stop the bleeding. It took weeks to heal and though she tended it regularly, it left two scars to remind us of that day. Dolores and I laugh about it now, because it's something we both remember, and there's much relief in the healing, love, and care behind it.

David was one kind-hearted person and a hard worker. He often took time to play with me and was my protector. He had a great sense of humor and he loved horses. One day when I came home from school, I found him lying on the sofa in pain. "Mother," I asked, "what happened to David?"

She said, "Unfortunately when he was grooming the horse, she misbehaved and kicked him." Mother reminded me to pray for him. Thankfully, it wasn't worse, though he was in pain for several days. I felt so sorry for him.

Mother told me that David was a great baseball player but my father wouldn't let him play because of religious reasons, which I had trouble making sense of. Maybe it had to do with that "showy side" they didn't want us to exhibit, or maybe it was because of competition and winning. Or even the uniform, had he been able to join the team. I never really understood it. David and I were nine years apart and even though we weren't close in age, his kindness stayed with me forever and we always felt close. After high school, he did volunteer work for a year. He got married and had two beautiful children shortly after that assignment.

One of the tragedies that David's kind heart had to bear was when his grown daughter experienced a fire in her house and it burned 60% of her body, creating excruciating pain and scarring. She died not long after, which was heartbreaking for the whole family. When David died several years later, I felt he died with a broken heart, and I wished there were some way I could have protected and comforted him like he did me.

Yvonne, was another of my beautiful sisters who followed Dolores's footsteps in helping with the chores. She never complained. I will always appreciate her alto voice when we sang while we worked together. She had a contented nature and enjoyed building a world of creativity in which to express her talents and skills. One of her talents was the art of flower arranging and after she left home, she became a florist and did a fantastic job for her customers. To this day she can build a flower arrangement fit for a queen!

When she got married and left our family circle, I cried. Right before she left, she gave me a gift. I opened it up and found a pair of brand new, beautiful, silky nylons. To this day I remind her how sweet that gesture was because it was a gift of thoughtfulness, girl to girl. It had more to do with passing the baton of womanhood than leaving me to take over her chores. She was, in her sweet way, supporting my own dreams of adulthood and independence. Yvonne got married right after high school and had four beautiful children. She and her husband enjoyed collecting antiques and managed the Green Acres Farm Bed and Breakfast for many years in Mt. Joy, Pennsylvania.

Karl was the fourth child, who had a golden voice. I told him, "You sing like Johnny Cash and Elvis Presley mixed together," and we both laughed. He never truly enjoyed farm life and struggled with walking the tightrope to keep my father pleased with him. I felt that Karl often lacked the positive support he needed around his own skills and talents, in that I believe he might have been a great singer if he'd pursued his talent professionally. Instead, he joined the Air Force, and I cried again when he left home. Later he married and had two beautiful children. Though he had a good life and sweet family, when Karl died at sixty-nine, we all felt he'd left us far too soon.

My oldest siblings joined the Mennonite Church, but Karl declared that for him, "It only lasted for a few days." That path was just not well-suited to his dreams. He was very thoughtful and kind, but some of the restrictions made him feel like he was not staying on the "straight and narrow path." As we know, joining the military forces was not supported by my parents and their church community, so it's easy to understand why he felt a need to step outside of the parameters he experienced at home. I know he made good choices that worked for him, and in my heart I feel he always did his very best. His spirit remains with me as a kind and thoughtful person, even during his years of military service.

I always felt fortunate to have older siblings but because of the age differences, it took a long time to get to know them. As I grew older, I discovered the goodness in each one and I treasure the memories we made. Girl, boy, girl, boy, and then I came along, followed by my two younger siblings whom I also hold dear.

# Radio Rules

*"Music gives a soul to the universe, wings to the mind,*
*flight to the imagination, and life to everything."* -Plato

While I was growing up, we didn't have a television set in our home, so our radio was my TV, and I believe it helped me to "see things" more visually and creatively. If I closed my eyes while I listened to music, I could imagine and daydream about what the words meant. Colorful images and emotional romance scenes appeared in my mind when I listened to songs like "That's Amore" by Dean Martin.

"Having a radio doesn't mean you can listen to anything you want," my parents announced. "We will be selective and listen to wholesome programs." Wholesome? At that time, I was too young to be able to spell much, so I giggled inside and could only think of Holsom bread, while trying to understand. "There are many Christian stations and wonderful gospel music," my parents said, "and that is what we will listen to."

Often, as I skipped along the sidewalk, arriving home from school, I could hear someone playing the radio in the house. It was my mother with her angelic voice, singing along with gospel songs, such as, "Amazing Grace," "In the Sweet By and By," and "Precious Memories." It was a highlight to hear music in my home, even though the selection of music was limited. Mother also played the piano, and it didn't take long for us to gather around and sing along with her.

Rock and roll and country music were off limits, so of course, this made me more than just curious about them. During my preteen and teenage years, when I was home alone, I would secretly tune in and listen to other kinds of music. Mostly I ended up listening to Dean Martin, Bing Crosby, and Frank Sinatra, to play it safe. I convinced myself their romantic songs were acceptable. You know how it goes when your parents say "No." I always wanted to know why I couldn't listen to rock and roll but it was unheard of to question my parents' authority. With the strict rules of my family's religion, there were many things off limits.

The radio made a big impression on me. It was a great communication tool and a force for social change during my youth. By listening to the words, I imagined what it might be like outside my sheltered life. The radio made my imagination run wild and forced me to ask questions. How did people really live in other homes and other countries? What kind of music did they listen to?

To this day I love to turn on the radio. Even when it's not on, I can still hear the programs of yesterday, and I only began to breathe freely when I realized much later that there is more than one station in life, and more than one kind of song that we can wholeheartedly enjoy.

# Mother's Hair Receiver

*"Hair is a beautiful form of self-expression."*
~Carolyn Aronson

I was born with black, curly hair. I can still hear people commenting, "Look at those beautiful curls!" As my hair grew longer, and before I started the first grade, Mother began braiding my hair. When she did this, the only place you could see my curls was at the ends of those braids.

When I was a young teenager, one of my chores was to clean the five rooms upstairs every Thursday. I had so much fun pretending that I lived on the second floor in an apartment. I loved cleaning my parents' bedroom because there is where I found interesting items like books on marriage and sex. Neither of these topics was discussed in our home, well, maybe once. However, the subject of women having long hair was an important issue that was discussed. Why? The Bible reads, "But if a woman have long hair, it is a glory to her: for her hair is given her for a covering." I Corinthians 11:15 King James Version.

Because of my parents' interpretation of the scriptures, we were never allowed to cut our hair, let alone let it hang freely and blow in the wind. We only left our hair down when we washed it and for bedtime. If we joined the church, we had to keep our glorified hair up in a bun and covered. I never understood all the fuss about women's long hair because most of the people I saw outside of our religious community wore their hair short and styled.

On top of Mother's dresser was her "hair receiver." Many people, especially the younger ones in this day and age, have never heard of a hair receiver and have no idea what it's for. Dating from the Victorian times through the early 1950s, hair receivers were placed on top of the dressing tables of most fashionable ladies. They were small, round dishes made of glass, metal, wood, ceramic, porcelain, or plastic. They came in different shapes, each with a lid on top. These lids almost always included a hole in the middle. After brushing their hair, women would collect any loose hairs, twist them around their fingers, and put them into the hair receiver for different reasons. Some would collect their hair to build what was called a "rat" or "ratt," which was a bundle of hair secured within a hairnet that could be invisibly incorporated into a hairstyle to give it volume. Sometimes people used hair for art projects, like floral designs framed in a glass case and displayed. Others, like my mother, collected and discarded it.

Mother's plastic hair receiver was a fun item for me to take care of on Thursdays. After she brushed her hair each day, she would clean her brush and wrap the loose hair around her finger, tucking it into the hair receiver through the hole of the lid. The fun began when I cleaned it out. I lined up the curls from her hair receiver around my hairline above my forehead and secured them with bobby pins. I loved pretending to be sophisticated and danced in front of the mirror admiring the beauty of her curls around my face.

I still have my mother's hair receiver, but I no longer have my long hair after I realized, as an adult, how much I enjoy wearing it short. To me, the hair receiver is symbolic: What we receive in life, we can learn from, play with, and then choose to let go of when it is no longer needed.

# Farm Life, City Life

*"The country habit has me by the heart."*
~Vita Sackville-West

While growing up on our farm in York County, Pennsylvania, during the 1950s, I discovered that living in the country was like night and day compared with living in the city. The smells of the country, such as wheat fields in July, and the honeysuckle that grew wild amidst the landscape were breathtaking. No one likes the smell of manure, but then I didn't like the smell of city fumes from cars, buses, and trucks, either. The country suited me fine even with the ripe smells of the good fertilizers we used in our farm communities.

We made regular trips to the city of York to sell our produce at the market, shop for necessities, and attend church. It wasn't unusual to hear prayers sent for good weather for our crops, which depended on rain and sunshine. My parents owned a forty-eight-acre vegetable farm. We had two Holstein cows, several large, white, Yorkshire pigs, a horse, dogs and cats, a donkey, and hundreds of Leghorn chickens. Gardening was an art, and my parents were pros at making beautiful vegetable and flower gardens. The long, straight rows of corn, peas, beans, carrots, lettuce, and tomatoes looked impressive. The tomatoes were grown for the Hanover Cannery. During tomato picking, we filled hundreds of baskets to load onto the tractor-trailer trucks for transporting.

There was always work to be done on the farm. In the mornings, Mother reminded us to get to work early outside, while the cool breeze lasted. We siblings were responsible for weeding the gardens, and by

August we would harvest. Mother, in her floral apron, would set about canning fruits and vegetables. She made sure she had plenty of quart-sized Ball mason jars with zinc lids, and she used a big blue Agate canner with a rack to put the jars in to process. Sharing how many jars she canned was a big deal when talking with her friends. She would proudly announce, "Today I canned thirty jars of peaches." I can still hear her joyfully shout, "And they all sealed!" Oh to hear the lids pop! For those who are not familiar with the canning process, "Most two-piece lids will seal with a 'pop' sound while they're cooling, as the lid gets sucked down by the vacuum created by the contents cooling and contracting inside the jar." (Retrieved from http://pickyourown.org/spoilage_testing.htm 9/17/18)

Selling vegetables near our house was a lot of fun. We spread the vegetables on a card table and people would often stop on their way home from work to buy. I had fun putting the vegetables in bags and receiving the money and giving change when necessary. I did not see roadside stands in the city, only in the city market. We delivered some of our vegetables to friends who sold them for us in the city market.

Singing together as a family while Mother played the piano was a weekly activity. Singing a cappella was a joy while doing our chores and to us it seemed natural. We often sat in a circle shelling beans or husking corn. The songs from church followed us home, "Heaven, Happy Home Above," "Amazing Grace," "Heavenly Sunshine," "Brighten the Corner Where You Are," and "Work for the Night is Coming" are just a few. Those songs were treasured, especially the one about work. Dad often plowed the fields when it was cool and dark, and if there wasn't work to be done outside, indeed there was always a list of things to do inside the house. We did not have an indoor bathroom until I was a teenager. Instead, we used an outhouse, which my dad always cleaned out each month. We had a chamber bucket in the house, and we children took turns taking it to the outhouse to dump. We were also in charge of cleaning that bucket at the faucet outside, and having it ready each night. This was not a fun chore but we did it! And we sang while doing it, sometimes making up songs that quietly protested having to do this chore!

Mother managed her colorful English flower gardens and grew the most beautiful ferns, daylilies, roses, snapdragons, bleeding heart, cockscomb, foxglove, hibiscus, hydrangea, and more. The hydrangea is especially memorable to me because as soon as the flowers started blooming each spring, Mother gave us children permission to go barefoot. "The earth is warming up," she told us. The flowerbeds reminded me of the color-wheel, and the fragrances beckoned me to stop and sniff the lavender and yellow roses.

When we went to the city, it was a big adventure for me. My eagle eyes were glued to the window observing how people lived. I was fascinated with how the red brick houses sat together in rows, block after block. Many cars were parked along the streets, and sometimes trash was seen in the gutters. The small yards with little grass seemed so limited compared to the large open spaces surrounding us in the country. City children were often seen playing on the sidewalks and sometimes in the streets.

For many households, having a Bissell or Hoover carpet sweeper was a luxury, so without one, we had to shake our rugs outside. Sometimes rugs were hung on wash lines and whipped silly with a rug beater to clear the dust. By now my older siblings were no longer living at home, so I had more chores to do. Any time I could make these chores creative and fun was a good time for me.

On one of our trips to the city, I saw a lady on the second floor of her house shaking rugs outside her window above the tin roof of her first floor. She was looking right over her shoulder and having a conversation with her next-door neighbor, who was inside her own home! Living in a single farmhouse was very different from a row house, where everyone lived elbow to elbow. I found that scene so humorous that I adopted it, and from then on, whenever I cleaned upstairs at home, I would open the window, shake out our rugs, and look over my shoulder to my right, pretending I was talking to my next-door neighbor inside her home. In our neighborhood or at our house it was customary to roll up the throw rugs and take them to the balcony to sweep or downstairs to shake them out. I don't remember seeing our neighbors cleaning rugs from a window, so this practice was wildly fun for me. Thanks Mother, for teaching us how to work and have fun!

Work never seemed to end, but that was our lifestyle. How did we find time to go to church at least three times a week? We all worked together and made it happen. Life was often difficult, but I loved the country and learned many useful lessons, even though some of them I imported from the city.

# Bucket in Flight

*"The embarrassment of a situation can, once you are over it, be the funniest time in your life. And I suppose a lot of my comedy comes from painful moments or experiences in life, and you just flip them on their head."* ~Miranda Hart

I wish I could sing to you about what happened one day, a song like the one about the hole in dear Liza's bucket, but the hole in my bucket was nothing like hers. And my misadventure was way worse, and ever so embarrassing.

During the 1950s, many homes did not have indoor bathrooms, including ours. The outhouses were lined up behind each home in our neighborhood. Most people used them during the day, but at night, especially when it was cold, we used a container in the house, which was called a chamber bucket. Most of them were white with red or black trim around the lid and on the wooden handle. We kept ours on the second floor of the house, in the corner of a small room, to provide a little privacy.

Living on a farm, we had plenty of chores to do and most were tolerable, and even fun. But the chore of having to empty the chamber bucket each day was the one least favored by all of us little helpers. Mother always encouraged us children to make a game out of our chores, but for this one, it was not really possible to make it any fun. We took turns emptying the chamber bucket, but that didn't make it any easier, knowing it would be a few days until it was our turn to do it again. Some things in life you just have to follow through on without thinking too much, just to get them done.

I didn't know there was anything that could make it worse than it already was until one morning I was helping to clean the upstairs and it was my turn to empty the chamber bucket. I had to carry it down a long flight of stairs, and I was slowly going down the steps with it when I heard my mother talking with someone in the kitchen. Our neighbor, Lou, had stopped by to buy some corn and they got to talking. I thought to myself, *There is no way I am going past a guest with this blessed chamber bucket*, and I snuck back to the landing at the top of the stairs. Somehow, upon reaching the landing, I tripped, and the bucket went flying down the stairs with you know what spattering all over the place. I wanted to die or crawl in a hole, but I couldn't do either. I hid behind the door of one of the bedrooms, and stood there ready to cry, when I heard Lou say goodbye to my mother.

Slowly I opened the door to the stairway below. Mother looked at me from the front door, and asked what had happened. Mortified, I said, "Come and see. Somehow I tripped and the bucket flew right out of my hands!" We both stood there gaping at the fantastically adorned staircase and walls and suddenly we started laughing like hyenas, knowing full well what we had to do. With a deep breath, she calmly asked me to go get a clean bucket of water and the mop. I said, "I sure wish we could bring in the hose and wash everything down the steps." Of course, that wasn't going to happen since we had wooden steps with carpet mats and wooden floors.

Mother said, "Make sure you fill the bucket with hot water and add some vinegar." She loved using vinegar to clean. We even used vinegar to clean the windows and make them sparkle. She said, "The quicker we get this cleaned up, the better it will be. Let's open some more windows and maybe the doors too, to let the air come through. Anything to get this place smelling good again!" We worked hard getting things cleaned up and continued to laugh. "Well," she said, "that is the first time that's ever happened and let's hope it's the last." Fortunately, it never happened again.

In *Confessions of a Shopaholic*, the woman says, "It's only embarrassing if you care what people think." Well, I certainly was thinking of the guest and my mother, and would've been morbidly embarrassed if the guest had been aware of what had happened. Thank goodness he left when he did! I am still amazed at how calmly my mother handled the situation. She never once said anything negative to me, like, "How stupid of you."

Mother was a great example of patience, understanding, and humor in helping me to overcome this very embarrassing experience. She broke the spell of mortification by laughing, and not at me, but with me. I often envied her cool disposition and wished I had more of it. Maybe I have more of her in me than I give myself credit for, like knowing how to laugh at my mistakes.

# Work for the Night is Coming

*"The best preparation for good work tomorrow is to do good work today.* ~Elbert Hubbard

"Good morning children, rise, and shine, please get up before the sun gets hot," my mother would daily request. "But isn't the sun always hot?" I chuckled to myself. She would always have a list of things for us to do every day, especially during the summer, when school was out. Growing up on a farm meant hard work and lots of it! The meaning of that word *work* brings to mind many associated descriptions, such as labor, toil, effort, performance, production, struggle, task, obligation, sweat, and daily grind. And it also brings to mind the beautiful old hymn:

> Work, for the night is coming,
> Work thro' the morning hours;
> Work while the dew is sparkling,
> Work 'mid springing flow'rs,
> Work when the day grows brighter,
> Under the glowing sun;
> Work for the night is coming,
> When man's work is done.

(Written in 1854 by Annie Louisa Walker, aka Mrs. Harry Coghill, retrieved from https://hymnary.org, 10/8/18)

I usually imagined my school friends were off to the pool for the day as I worked. "Sandra, you can pull weeds in the garden or help plant tomatoes," my mother said one day. My two younger siblings followed me around like little spring chickens and I didn't mind. My mother often said, "It's great to see you children working together without quarreling," and most of the time that was true.

When we were old enough, planting tomatoes was an adventure and somewhat fun, because it was such a big job each new season. One of us drove the tractor while two others sat in separate seats on the planting machine. As the machine made a hole in the ground, each took turns putting a tomato plant into the hole, one at a time. The water flowed in with the plant and the machine closed the dirt over the roots. The driver had to go at the same speed the whole time while the plants were placed in the ground, in rhythm. Sometimes one of us got to ride on top of the water tank just for fun.

My dad would always ask, "Are you sure you filled the water tank?" "Yes," I could always reply, quite certain. There was no way we wanted to be in the middle of the field without water for the plants. I loved watching how the machine worked. The device made planting much easier than putting one plant in the ground at a time while scuffling around on your knees. The straight rows looked beautiful, and after ten acres were planted, we prayed for rain and sunshine to help the plants grow. The song we sang still rings in my ears:

Work, for the night is coming,
Work thro the sunny noon;
Fill brightest hours with labor—
Rest comes sure and soon.

And sometimes rest felt like it did not come soon enough. Fortunately, my mother would have a delicious three-course homemade meal ready for lunch. We often had mashed potatoes with lots of homemade butter, tender, juicy beef or chicken, a vegetable, and some kind of dessert like rice pudding, or sponge cake with strawberries on top. Her meals were to die for. I remember feeling tired and energized at the same time as we ate. If it was a sweltering hot day, we were allowed to take a siesta under our favorite maple shade tree for about an hour or spray each other with the water hose. That time always went by way too fast, and soon Mother would call, "Children, it's time to get back to work. Please make sure the animals are fed first, before you go out to the garden."

Feeding the animals was a great way to learn about their behaviors. For example, the pigs and hogs came to their food trough with dirty faces, snorting and eating like, well, pigs! Chickens lined up along the feeders the minute their trays were filled with food and water. I often imagined they were showing thanks to God because right after they drank, they raised their heads and looked upward.

The cows chewed their food over and over. Sometimes I wondered why they took so long to eat. Later I read that cows spend nearly eight hours a day chewing their cud. After the cow swallows, the rumen muscles send the cud back up to the cow's mouth, and it is re-chewed and swallowed again, and then it goes to their stomach to squeeze out all of the moisture and nutrients. Now that is a real exercise.

Animals are fascinating to watch, and sadly, I often compared people to animals. "Mother, today at school I saw Frank 'eating like a pig.' He slobbered and licked his fingers. It was a disgusting sight." "Well, all children are taught differently or not taught at all, so please don't make fun of others," she gently admonished, as I smacked my lips like a pig and giggled.

This song ends with the following verse:

Work, for the night is coming,
Under the sunset skies:
While their bright tints are glowing,
Work for the daylight flies.
Work till the last beam fadeth,
Fadeth to shine no more;
Work, while the night is dark'ning,
When man's work is o'er.

And just as the words circle around, so do the day and night.

My parents took the scriptures and songs such as this one literally. "For even when we were with you, this we commanded you, that if any would not work, neither should he eat." 2 Thesalonians 3:10. Kings James Version

Under the influence of many scriptures, hymns, and gospel songs, I tried to take the positive ideas with me. I am convinced that one of the reasons I thrive on good, hard work is because of these influences in my upbringing. Later in life, I learned that I can create a nice balance between work and relaxation, but it will always be a challenge for me to be truly comfortable relaxing for too long. I find comfort in knowing there are two sides to everything, as the song implies. It depends on what you want to emphasize or prioritize.

I have no regrets about learning all kinds of work, which I generally have always tackled with great enthusiasm. I am thankful that I've been motivated to work but the key element is to keep a good balance.

# The Life of Butter

*"Life isn't life without real butter."* -A. D. Posey

Do you ever stop and think where food comes from? Like vegetables, fruit, and yes, butter? How does butter get from the store to your table? Today it is so easy to go to a grocery store and buy all different kinds of butter. Even in ancient times, the value of butter was much appreciated, as shown in Judges 5:25 of the King James Version, where it says butter was brought to the king "in a lordly dish." Did you ever wonder where the magic begins, and what it takes to see it placed in front of you?

Growing up on a farm, I quickly learned where our food came from, and I often participated in its journey from field to table. My mother proudly displayed an array of various dishes at her table, from veggies to fruits, and plenty of homemade butter, and jams. The butter glowed like sunshine. Her kitchen routines were fascinating to watch and learn about, and the food was always fresh, wholesome, and savory. I loved when she browned butter in a mini frying pan and poured it over the vegetables and mashed potatoes. My taste buds always asked for more.

Our farm was a vegetable and chicken farm, with only a few cows, bulls and a horse. We no longer had a dairy farm like we had in Millport, but we knew if we had a couple of cows they would provide us with milk and butter. To learn about the life of butter, we have to start right from the beginning, with the cow. For us, it was essential to know how much our cows needed to eat to provide good milk. "The average cow can consume over 100 pounds of feed per day." (Retrieved from http://www.

dairymoos.com/how-much-do-cows-eat/ 01/11/19) Our cows were grass-fed and sometimes given grains and silage made from cornstalks.

Before a cow can start producing milk, she must have delivered a calf. Then the mother and calf are separated within a few days so that along with the milk she produces for her calf, there is extra for other uses, such as milk and butter for the family. The calf is fed from a large bottle with a nipple or from a bucket of milk. I always thought that was a cruel act when the calf was taken away from her mother. It is very stressful on the cow and the calf to be separated. The cow will continue to produce milk, but, if she becomes pregnant again, she will be milked until her 7th month only, out of a gestation period of nine months, so she can build up good nutrition for her new calf. Today with modern technology, dairy cows are bred specially to produce large quantities of milk. During my youth, my parents or older siblings milked our cows by hand, twice a day.

We brought the milk in from the barn and put it in sizeable wide-mouth gallon jars with lids, to cool in the refrigerator for one or two days while the cream rose to the top. "Cream" is actually the fat from the milk. We usually got one or two cups of cream from each jar. We were cautious about keeping things clean because we did not pasteurize our milk. Before we put the cream in the wooden churn, we made sure it was spotless and washed with boiling water. The smell of the cream reminded me of cooked sweet corn.

After putting the cream in the wooden churn, someone had to turn the handle to make the butter. There is a blade inside the churn connected to the handle outside. My youngest sister and I had the responsibility to take care of this chore. So naturally, we made a game out of the routine. "So you think you can beat me?" I asked my younger sister, as we got ready to make butter one afternoon. "Sure," she said. I turned the handle on the wooden churn 100 times, which took a while, and then yelled, "It's your turn!" She did a great job trying to beat me. We took turns until the cream got thick and turned into butter. By then our arms felt like dangling rubber bands. Turning usually took about 35-40 minutes.

We drained the liquid from the butter through a muslin cloth and watched the color turn from pale white to a lemon-yellow glow as our churning firmed it up. Once it was done, we eagerly put the thick butter into a wooden rectangle-shaped mold, which held precisely one pound of butter. We had a mold set and we imprinted each block of butter with a design. The imprint on our mold looked like a delicate bouquet of violets. We were so proud of the end result, every single time. Since we were a large family, our butter did not last long but, if we had extra, we would wrap it in wax paper and freeze it to use later. The molded imprint of beautiful violets on the butter was the sign that the chore was almost finished.

At the dinner table one night, my sister said, "Guess what mother! I turned the handle on the butter churn nearly 100 times!" "Don't stretch it," I said, "maybe it was closer to fifty." "Now girls," my mother said, "it doesn't matter, because what's important is that you got the job done."

My sister and I were Mother's big helpers. Mother was thrilled to have enough butter to last for a few more days. Eating the butter that we made was a family celebration.

The whole chore wasn't finished, though, until we cleaned the wooden butter churn. After setting the butter into the mold, we hauled the heavy churn to the sink to be washed thoroughly with boiling water. We took off the lid and disconnected the handle and the metal blade inside. We washed everything in hot soapy water and then rinsed it with boiling water, and put it out in our pantry to dry. Ready to use for the next time!

Participating in "the life of butter" gave me an appreciation for what it took to enjoy the luxury of fresh butter at my fingertips.

Karoline 2019

# Barefoot Season

*"I'm actually a barefoot girl."* -Elle King

I couldn't wait for spring and summertime, my favorite months of the year. On our farm in the backyard the smell of fresh cut grass, honeysuckle, blooming phlox, and roses was always welcome. "Mother," I asked, "when may I go barefoot?" "Not until the snowball bushes bloom," she said. "But it's warm enough I want to go now," I said. "No, the ground is still damp and you might get sick," she always reminded me. The snowball bush (hydrangea) is slower to bloom than the other flowers, which I thought was unfair.

At the first sign of the snowball blooms, my shoes were off and I went barefoot for the rest of the summer. It felt so freeing to run through the grass, mud puddles, and in the garden without shoes. I can still feel the dirt under my feet and between my toes. I declared that I was part of the earth and appreciated the feel. Freedom was limited in my home, but somehow going barefoot felt very disentangling.

One of the fun games we children played was to see who could be the first to run back and forth across the stones on our lane without yelling that it hurt. Early in the season, we would take turns walking in slow motion back and forth, sometimes being in severe pain, as we walked barefoot on the sharp stones. Then, like a switch, our feet had toughened up and we were running back and forth across the stones without complaining. The simple joys of summer came in many forms.

We did not have a lot of "things" to play with on the farm, so it was common for us to create our own fun. Playing games like hide and seek and tag were just a few of our amusements. Going barefoot was what most of us children did growing up on a farm. But keep in mind there are two sides to every story; there is fun, and then there is sometimes pain.

"Mother, I just got stung by bees in the yard," I cried one day. And she quickly said, "Let's put some baking soda or vinegar on it." Sure enough, either one worked in minutes to take away the pain and swelling. Another remedy was to put mud on the sting if you could find a mud puddle. The mud keeps it closed, which keeps it from getting infected. It cools and reduces swelling, plus eases the pain. To this day I am a firm believer in using mud to take away the pain of an insect bite or sting. As an adult, I stepped on a nest of bees on the ground and got stung multiple times. Fortunately, there was a mud puddle near-by, and I stuck my foot in the mud. HA! It eased the pain and helped it to heal. Also, if I accidentally stepped on a rusty nail or when I got a splinter in my foot when I went barefoot, it wasn't fun, but that did not stop me. Getting my tetanus shot wasn't fun either, but it didn't hurt any worse than a bee sting.

Did you know there are benefits to going barefoot? According to Dr. Isaac Eliaz, in his article "The Surprising Health Benefits of Going Barefoot," "walking barefoot, also known as 'earthing,' has gone from being a kooky counter-culture trend to a scientifically-researched practice with some remarkable health advantages, such as increasing antioxidants, reducing inflammation, and improving sleep." Earthing has to do with walking barefoot on natural surfaces, such as soil, grass, or sand. The "benefits come from the relationship between our bodies and the electrons in the earth." (Retrieved from https://www.mindbodygreen.com/0-9099/the-surprising-health-benefits-of-going-barefoot.html 01/15/2019.)

Little did I know how good it was, health-wise, for me to go barefoot, I just loved the freedom. To this very day, I like keeping in step without shoes. If I had it my way, that would be most of the time.

# The Flying Donkey

*"You might have seen a housefly, maybe even a superfly,*
*but I bet you ain't never seen a donkey fly!"*
~Eddie Murphy in *Shrek*

Bible stories shared in Sunday school and by my mother are stamped in my mind to this day. I loved hearing the Bible story about Jesus riding the donkey into Jerusalem and seeing the pictures that went with it. People came running to greet him with palm branches, and some took off their coats and put them on the ground to show respect. In the Bible, the donkey was used for ceremonial purposes and symbolized peace. Kings would come riding upon a horse when they were interested in war, but rode the donkey when seeking peace.

While I was growing up, it was very popular for our Sunday school teachers to use flannel boards to tell a story. It was a way to show a little action as the teacher floated the characters, animals, and landscapes around on the board. I always enjoyed it, especially if the teacher showed enthusiasm! She would say, "Can you imagine Jesus riding on a donkey on roads that were not paved?" Then she would bounce the flannel donkey up and down, and we children were pulled right into the story amidst a chorus of giggles. And our teacher would describe how when Mary and Joseph were looking for a place to stay, riding on a donkey, what a challenge it must have been in the dark without any headlights!

I loved having a younger brother and sister, Delmar and Dawn. They were so much fun to babysit and play games with, like hide and seek, softball, and badminton. We also loved being outside at twilight, racing around the yard, and catching lightning bugs! My youngest brother Delmar is a gem, kind-hearted and giving. Sometimes you don't see that in a person until you get to know them.

One day I decided I wanted to take a ride out to the orchard on our donkey. I was feeling fearless and confident that day. Our donkey looked like the kind I saw in the Bible pictures but we did not have a donkey on the farm for the reasons described in ancient times. Our donkey was there only to feed, ride, and look at. He was small enough for me to hop right on and tamer than a house cat! I remember holding onto his mane and feeling very secure as we took off, although I was not using a saddle. His speed was perfect for me because donkeys rarely go fast! My goal was to check the harvest of the black walnut trees to see if any walnuts had fallen on the ground for us to pick up. We arrived safely, and I was thrilled the donkey listened to my commands.

The black walnut harvest was a big project for us in the fall. We would pick the walnuts off the ground and put them in a wheelbarrow and haul them to our driveway. My mother usually was in charge of driving over them in our car to take off the outer green shells. What a mess they made! If we did not wear gloves and we picked them up, our hands got stained black. After the green shells were removed, we put the walnuts in flat containers and took them to our attic to dry. During the winter, we would sit around the table and hammer the hard, brown shell off, to pick out the beautiful walnuts so we could use them for baking. It was a tough job, but Mother always made it easier by starting a song that we knew. We sang like a flock of birds in harmony.

Soon, it was time to return from the orchard to the barn on the donkey. The ride was going smoothly, so slow, it made me sleepy, but all was well until we got to the corn crib and my dear brother Delmar suddenly jumped out from the corn crib and yelled, "Hey!" The blessed donkey reared up on his hind legs so high that I flipped over his head and onto the ground. The donkey flew towards the barn while I sat there with my skirt over my shoulders, trying to pull myself together. I remember yelling to Delmar, "I'm telling Mother!" but he just ran off laughing as I picked myself up and told the donkey he could have been a whole lot steadier, which was rather a joke, since the episode scared us both.

I never heard any stories about Jesus or other Bible characters being thrown off their donkeys, but I would imagine they had their moments as well. What I do know after that episode is that flying donkeys exist. To this day, my brother and I laugh about that time in our childhood when he played this prank, and I knew he meant no harm. He had no idea that donkeys could fly. For each birthday, ever since, he receives a different card from me with a picture of a donkey looking him right in the face. HA! Having a younger brother is treasure!

# My Little Sister

*"A sister is a little bit of childhood that can never be lost."*
~Marion C. Garretty

I've always loved music, and especially music for children. During the 1940s and 1950s, it was so much fun when my mother bought records to share with the family. The records came in three speeds, vinyl 45-rpm, the 78-rpm, and the 33 1/3-rpm records. I loved when she purchased the 45-rpm records. Sometimes they came in different colors like red, and yellow. We had many children's songs, with religious, and fun themes. The 45-rpm records had a song on each side and even though we bought it for the one song we were always eager to hear the song on the other side. We were usually pleasantly surprised.

We had this one 45-rpm red record and on one side the song was called "Me Too." It was a catchy tune, and it wasn't long before my little sister Dawn and I had it memorized. It was a perfect song because my sister often wanted to do what I did. She was a fun sister and very helpful.

If I went to the store, Dawn would say, "Me too." If I went to gather eggs, she would say, "Me too." If I hopped on the tractor, she would beg to ride along. Of course, that was risky because I was known to drive too fast. One time, when I was 13 years old, I said, "Dawn would you like to go for a ride on the tractor?" She said, "Yes, me too!" and jumped on the back and stood up on the edge of the frame while holding onto the seat. Off we went laughing in the wind. All of a sudden, I was going around the corner way too fast and noticed that instead of being on all four wheels we were up on two. Fortunately, I managed to get the tractor under control, and neither of us were thrown off. That might have been the beginning of when she started to be more selective about what she wanted to do with me.

One of my proudest days was when we fifth graders were allowed to bring one of our siblings to school. I asked my mother, "May I take Dawn along with me to school next week? The teacher said we're having a day to invite one of our siblings." Mother smiled and said, "Yes, as long as you make sure she stays with you." I enjoyed the adventure as much as Dawn did. She looked beautiful in her yellow dress, white socks, and black patent leather shoes. She looked like a princess from the farm, and I was so happy to tell everyone she was my little sister. It certainly was a "Me too" day. She often watched me get on the bus and wanted to go along, and now it came true.

The joys of childhood were many, even though we had our challenges. As I pen this story, I am reminded again there is a reason for those who came into my life. Whether it is family members or friendships along the way, we learn from those relationships. I was taught responsibility and to show kindness to my little sister. That was a great practice on my journey in life.

The words to the five-verse children's song "Me Too" will always be a treasure, and remind me that it is a gift to have a little sister.

# The Silver Spoon

*"When you do not forgive you magnify the hurts you have received, but blame the other for the pain you now cause yourself."* ~William Fergus Martin

It's interesting to me how traditions are carried down from one generation to another, and I love learning about the history behind them. I remember mother showing me the silver spoon I received when I was a baby and then when my husband and I had our daughters, sure enough, I blessed each child with her own silver spoon. These are treasured heirlooms passed down through the generations of our family.

Originally the phrase was "born with a silver spoon in his mouth," and it appeared in print in English as early as 1719, referring to the British aristocracy. The meaning of this phrase is to be "born into wealth and privilege." (Peter Anthony Motteux's translation of the Novel *Don Quixote* Retrieved from https://en.wikipedia.org/wiki/Silver_spoon 11/14/18)

"The earliest spoons were made of wood. The word *spoon*, derived from the Anglo-Saxon word *spon*, 'a chip of wood.'" As Robert Hendrickson states, "Every man is not born with a silver spoon in his mouth. Not everybody is born to wealth." "A silver spoon is a traditional gift given by godparents when the baby is born." (From the *Encyclopedia of Word and Phrase Origins* by Robert Hendrickson, Facts on File, New York, 1997. Retrieved from https://www.phrases.org.uk/bulletin_board/12/messages/931.html, 11/14/18)

Sandra L. Miller

Another theory I discovered regarding this quote, and maybe another reason why silver spoons were given, was that silver promotes good health because it disrupts bacteria cells and prevents disease.

Silver has been used to preserve food and water, and silver spoons became popular in the Middle Ages to protect against the plague. The wealthy could afford silver and escaped the worst ravages of the disease. In England, only 25% of the rich died during the epidemic of the 14th century while for peasants the death rate was 40-50%, according to Norman F. Cantor, in his book *In the Wake of the Plague*.

It was also known that the settlers in the American West used silver dollars in jugs of milk to keep the milk from spoiling. Silver nitrate drops have been used in newborn babies' eyes to prevent infection after birth. Today physicians and surgeons agree on the benefits of silver, and some say it can even heal wounds, but with the growth in popularity of antibiotics, silver is less commonly used for health.

I was not born into a wealthy family, but I certainly had my basic needs met. I wore hand-me-downs, handmade clothing, and occasionally got brand new shoes at the five and dime store. That was part of my life growing up. To get a silver spoon when I was born, made me chuckle later, as I did the research. "But why did we receive a silver spoon when we were born?" I think my mother's wish was that the silver spoon would bring us good health and good fortune. I treasure it because it was from her and she enjoyed tradition.

While growing up on the farm, it was typical for our family to share the chores. We had house chores, farm chores, and yard chores plus more. Most days, near dinnertime, my mother would say, "Sandra, please set the table, while I prepare the food." Very diligently I would clean off the table, choose the plates, glasses, and the silverware. Usually, there would be seven of us at the table, since two of the oldest children had married and moved away.

Like most families, we siblings sometimes had our squabbles. Getting mad at our parents or siblings happens in every household, but we were never allowed to talk back to our parents or openly express hostility towards our siblings. Showing anger or complaining was not allowed, even though at times we were boiling underneath. We did not discuss our feelings or have a chance to explain our point of view, so sometimes I found my way around these restraints.

One day I was feeling angry with one of my siblings, quarreling over who had to do a particular chore. "No, he said, it's your turn to mow the lawn." I said, "No way, I just did it last week." As I was setting the table, I realized I could exercise a measure of spite without being discovered. As I came to my brother's place at the table, I carefully put the fork on the left side of the plate and the knife and spoon on the right side. I had a selection of spoons to choose from, which included some silver spoons with very thin, sharp edges, and some smooth flatware spoons. I always preferred using the smooth flatware. For me, the thin edges of the silver spoons were so sharp they interfered with eating and enjoying the food. If I were mad at someone, I would make sure I put a sharp silver spoon beside his or her plate. *Sorry brother,* I thought to myself with a secret smile, *it's your turn for this ugly, sharp spoon.* No one knew of this little "devil made me do it" trick until I got much older and confessed what I did. Of course, I had to come clean because I felt guilty!

As a preteen and teenager, I experienced challenges as all teenagers do. What made it more difficult for me was the religious dogma my family held to, and the resulting restriction on freedom of all kinds. I suppressed a lot of my feelings and frustrations until later in life. We each handle our challenges differently while growing up. I went along with what was expected out of fear and disapproval from my parents and sometimes that felt like punishment!

The useful lessons that I took with me from those years are: I am glad I was taught right from wrong, I appreciate learning good manners and a well-developed sense of etiquette, like how to set a beautiful table, and how to be respectful. Obviously, I was not being respectful in deliberately choosing to put an ugly, sharp silver spoon beside someone's plate, but for me, acting out in a subtle way made me feel good and provided some relief from what sometimes boiled inside.

Today, you are always welcome at our table and most certainly you will receive a smooth edged spoon. The spoon became symbolic for me. I learned what is important in life and that not being vengeful goes a long way toward happiness for all!

*"Showing off is the fool's idea of glory."* ~Bruce Lee

Showing Off
By Sandra L. Miller

Four children were born
And then there was one more.

Each child was unique and beautiful
Never staying still always moveable.

The fifth child grew up to be a show off at times
Everyone wondered why and looked for signs.

One time during her preteen years and being forward
She took a small plunger and stuck it to her forehead.

Around the room she went making everyone laugh
The plunger handle bobbled without breaking in half.

Off went the plunger and as she pulled
A circle was stamped and secured.

The next day she begged not to go to school
For on her forehead was an impression of a fool.

# The Susquehanna River

*"You have to expect things from yourself before you can do them."*
~Michael Jordan

The Susquehanna is a significant river located in the northeastern U.S. It is the longest river on the East Coast and drains into the Atlantic Ocean by way of the Chesapeake Bay. The name Susquehanna comes from the Delaware Iroquois language, and means "Oyster River."

When I was growing up, we did not have a swimming pool or a pond to cool off in, just a tub we filled with water to splash in like ducks. It didn't stop there. We often used the hose and ran around spraying cold water on each other. But on some hot summer days, the real treat was when my mother surprised us by announcing, "Let's make a picnic and go to the river." We would jump into our mother's handmade bathing suits and get all excited for the adventure.

We helped prepare her extraordinary picnics, which included a garden of food. We loved her homemade German potato salad, pickles, chicken sandwiches, and her delicious tapioca pudding.

One hot summer afternoon, we took off in our turquoise Pontiac and drove to the Susquehanna River, only five miles away. The setting was beautiful. The muddy, stony riverbanks were lined with beautiful old oak trees, and there was no sand to play on, but there was an old wooden raft that people dove from into the water. Mother found a grassy area where we could put the blanket and tablecloth for the picnic. After our picnic, we gradually waded into the river.

Looking back, I realize that it was a rather unsafe place for children because of the strong currents in the water that surprised you if you went out too far. No one mentioned wearing life jackets, and there was no lifeguard to look out for us. We were so innocent and none of us knew how to swim. Mother watched us, but she didn't know how to swim either, so if anything happened, we were on our own. She trusted us to use our common sense and stay close to the banks.

But of course, I was always testing my boundaries. I remember that on this day, I was hanging onto the wooden raft and then letting go to see how far out I could go and still manage to tread water. I went out farther and farther each time until that one dreadful moment when I got caught in a current. I can still feel the pull of the water and the struggle of trying to get back to the raft without having to yell for help. Finally I made it back to the raft again, but it was terrifying to experience having little control since I had no idea how to swim. I think Jesus must have been looking out for me as mother sometimes reminded me He did.

In those days we did so many risky things without thinking of the dangers. We'd hop in the car without seatbelts. It wasn't until after the mid-1960s that seatbelts became commonplace in motor vehicles. We jumped into the river regardless of the currents, without wearing life jackets or knowing how to swim. And we ran barefoot over gravel paths and through high grass, not knowing or caring what dangers might be hiding there.

One of the lessons I took with me from that experience was to make sure our children took swimming lessons early in life. Because of my scary experience, I always had huge respect for the powerful energy of water, especially in uncultivated, wild places, such as the river, which can be much more dangerous than a supervised swimming pool. I learned to use common sense but tried not to over-protect. As children, we loved the times when we had a chance to play freely, but looking back from adulthood, I really think the guardian angels were watching over us. Life is full of currents like the river. It takes strength and courage to tread through the challenges.

# The Manhunt

*"I believe that every single event in life happens in an opportunity to choose love over fear."* ~Oprah Winfrey

Not much happened in our small town of Starview, but every now and then, something dramatic occurred! Like the night someone broke into the Country Store and tried to rob the dear storeowner. It was after midnight when the robber entered the store. The storeowner, Mary, woke up to a strange sound and decided to go and check. She came out from her kitchen into the store with a baseball bat and threatened him, yelling, "I will use this bat if you don't leave right away!" She assumed it was a young guy not very experienced with robbing. My dad said, "Mary was very frightened, but was a brave soul and scared him away." We cheered for her, but it was scary for a young child to hear what had happened right across the street.

Another time a little 4-year-old girl in the neighborhood went missing. Everyone was in a panic and neighbors were asked to help with the search. My dad came into the house and said, "We have to help look for her!" So we all joined in the search. Thankfully, she was found, sound asleep near her home in a neighbor's baby crib. My mother said, "The guardian angel had to be watching over her."

The most dramatic event that I remember happened when I was ten years old. One morning my dad came in from the barn after doing the chores and said, "I saw someone sitting in our car, sleeping." The car hadn't been put in the garage the night before and was parked near the main road unlocked. Of course, we all were scared and wondered who this man was. By the time my dad reported it to the police, the man was no longer in the car. I was afraid and worried, but my dad seemed to have things under control at the time. So, I hoped.

It wasn't long after the police were notified that two lawmen showed up at our kitchen door. They were dressed in long, tan coats and wore fancy hats. There was a loud knock, and my mother went to see who was there. As usual, Mother was very calm as she talked with the men, from behind the closed screen door. I saw her slowly lock it. I remember clinging to my mother's apron as she spoke to the two men. "Yes," she said, "the man was in the car this morning, but the last time we checked he was gone." They were very professional, as they said who they were and then showed their FBI badges. I could see they carried guns, which really made me nervous. One FBI agent explained that they were looking for a convict who had escaped from a prison, only an hour from where we lived. He had escaped from the psychiatric ward.

They said, "Stay in the house, lock all the doors, and don't answer the door if a stranger shows up." The men met my dad out in the barn where we stored the bales of straw and grains. This is where we children often played, and I was thinking how eerie it was that someone might be hiding there. The more I thought about it, the more I realized it would be a great place for a prisoner on the run to hide.

After about an hour, the FBI agents came out of the barn. Not three men but four! One man was handcuffed. It was difficult to see them as they put him in the back seat of their car. They thanked my dad for his help and drove off.

You can imagine what the conversation was like at the dinner table that evening. My dad said, "Those guys were pros. They inched their way into the barn and tiptoed on top of the straw bales. They walked and then stopped, listening as they scanned the bales of straw with a flashlight. It was a very tedious job, and they knew if they were patient and quiet they would be able to see any movement."

As they called out, "Anyone there?" they would freeze and wait. After about forty-five minutes they were almost ready to call it quits. But they kept going until they came to a pile of loose straw. One agent thought he heard something but wasn't sure because there were animals making noises in the barn below. They stood and waited. The other agent pointed to the loose straw where he was sure he saw movement. They had to be very cautious because they still didn't know for sure. Was the escaped prisoner under our haystack?

They slowly began to clear the straw away from around the edge of the mound. They didn't know if this person was armed, so they had to be very careful how they moved the straw, in case he was there. Just as they were ready to move more straw, they saw movement and a man slowly stood up in the middle of the straw mound. The FBI men had their guns ready, but fortunately, he willingly surrendered. He looked very sweaty and frightened. He seemed disoriented and confused. Slowly they handcuffed him, as he mumbled, "I didn't harm anyone!"

My dad said, "The FBI agents thanked me for my help and said they would return the convict to the prison." They also said, "This man had a metal plate put in his head, and this is not the first time he escaped." "Mother," I asked, "what does it mean to have a metal plate put in his head?" She said, "It is a flat plate used to cover serious defects of the skull, after major trauma." I cringed and said, "I think that would be very uncomfortable."

This was not an ordinary episode that took place in our small town. You can be sure the story flew like wildfire and was often discussed when people came to our country store. It didn't take long for the whole neighborhood to hear about what had happened.

As I reflect, I'm impressed with how my parents kept their cool, had faith in those who came to help, and were thankful no one got hurt. A child never forgets those moments and remembers the strength and love of others.

# Sunday Afternoons

*"Sunday clears away the rust of the whole week."*
~Joseph Addison


Our town consisted of only 100 people, two churches, one gas station, a barbershop, a one-room schoolhouse, and a country store. In a way, the community felt like one big family, and everyone knew each other, like the town of Mayberry in the old *Andy Griffith Show* on TV.

Our family faithfully attended church, so much so, that I thought we practically lived there. We went Wednesday night to prayer meeting, Saturday night for youth meetings, Sunday morning for Sunday school and a sermon, and Bible school the last two weeks of summer and two weeks during the winter. Our music was always a cappella singing without a piano or any instruments. The harmony of the voices was next to heaven to listen to.

I was an ordinary child who wanted to live life to its fullest. However, because of our strict religion and parents, my childhood experiences were not always easy or pleasant.

Fortunately, I made friends quickly through the public school that I attended, which was my salvation. But I always felt I had to figure out how to live in two worlds. Living by the church rules meant that I was not allowed to participate in many activities at school, plus I wasn't free to roam around the neighborhood.

My mother was caught up in the church's expectations as well, but thankfully she was more gentle-spirited with me than my dad. She would always encourage me to think positively and be creative. I was not a rebellious child, but definitely one who wanted to be like my friends. To be of real help felt wonderful, but being creative felt even more critical to me.

On Sunday afternoons, most of the older people in our community took naps after lunch, or visited with friends and the children were expected to find something acceptable to do. My siblings and I were generally not allowed to interact with the neighborhood kids who were not Mennonite, but I was allowed to spend time with girlfriends from church. Or, if my parents approved of one of my friends from school, and if they knew the family, I could ask them to our house for a visit.

One of my "parentally approved" best girlfriends from school was Catherine Bell, from the nearby small town of Saginaw. She lived in a lovely house with beautiful landscaping. Sometimes on Sunday afternoons, she came to our place, and we played in the barn. We considered this acceptable activity, but if my parents had supervised, I'm not sure that would be the case. We would swing on the ropes attached to the rafters, way up high, from one beam to another, like monkeys, and then jump into thick, soft mounds of straw below.

"Catherine," I said one Sunday afternoon, "let's go higher the next time and see if we can land on the high beam." She was a little apprehensive, but off we flew. If we fell, we would land on top of the soft straw bales, so we knew it was "safe." She declared, after several soft landings, "Now that was loads of fun!"

When we got tired of swinging, we made tunnels with the straw bales. We were both scared to death to go through our tunnels because it was pitch dark inside and we didn't have a flashlight to use. Our goal was to get to the other end of a tunnel without panicking and backing up. If she went first, I always felt safer and followed. We usually made it out and cheered.

Sometimes we opened the hay hole in the loft and jumped down to where the feeders were for the cows and bull. This was definitely a bit sideways of safe and acceptable activity, because I remember how we would tease the bull and make him angry, then sit there and laugh ourselves silly. Catherine loved to come to the farm because she enjoyed being around animals, which she wasn't used to, being a "town girl."

When Catherine came to visit, I remember how we talked about school and discussed our teachers, those we liked and those we didn't.

We'd laugh and laugh about the silly things we did at school, like trying to get out of gym class. We never liked the vaulting horse. As for subjects, I was always grateful for how she helped me with math, a subject I never enjoyed. Church life was a big topic sometimes, and I usually complained about how difficult it was to have to be, and look, so different. I'd tell her I thought Lutherans seemed to have it easy and we'd laugh and laugh some more.

If I was lucky, my mother let me visit Catherine. I was thrilled to get away from the farm and visit her house. I still can see her parents, especially her father, a tiny, short, kindhearted and soft-spoken man. I remember the dark wood trim in the house and their small kitchen. But most of all, I remember how thrilled I was to be able to watch their TV. I couldn't wait to watch TV since we did not have one. It was funny how she seemed bored watching TV, while I was on the edge of my seat watching! Farm life sure was different from her lifestyle, and the joy was to appreciate the differences.

Sunday afternoons were filled with the freedom to read, write letters, and sometimes visit with friends. For Catherine and me, Sunday afternoons were like a breath of fresh air, no matter whose house we chose for our visit.

# Once When No One Was Looking

*"Everything is funny, as long as it's happening to somebody else." ~*
Will Rogers

I was thirteen years old and old enough to know better. My parents taught from the Holy Book, and I was drilled in right from wrong regularly, from the very beginning of my life. Churchgoers we were, Wednesday, Saturday, and Sunday nights, and Sunday mornings too.

One Saturday night, we visited a church called the North Hartman Street Mennonite Church. This church was small, with crystal glass windows that you could not see through. Stained glass windows were generally not found in Mennonite churches.

I remember sitting on very hard benches listening to another long sermon and kneeling for prayer more than I thought necessary. We were too young to understand most of what was being said, and I confess that all this kneeling, for me, meant time for muffled giggles with my friend who sat beside me and was also in need of amusement. Sometimes the prayers were so long we had time to play tic-tac-toe. I'm sure if Mother had noticed she would have reminded me to be more respectful, but we made sure we didn't sit too close to her.

At home, I remember Mother called the devil "Spotty" when we would do something wrong. "Sandra," she would chide, "I believe Spotty made you say that," whenever I misspoke. I have no idea where she got the name, but she liked saying it. HA!

Attendance was large the night we visited the North Hartman church, which meant the songs were louder than ever, thank goodness. A cappella singing is rich in tone and harmony. To hear the singing in this small church added much beauty and helped to relieve the monotony of sermons and prayers for us young people. Some of the men bellowed out the bass notes as though they were singing on stage.

People chose the range to sing according to their most comfortable, natural voice, such as bass, tenor, alto, or soprano. That is when I remember learning to sing alto because I couldn't always hit the high notes singing soprano, which was embarrassing for a while until I learned my voice range. I never bellowed out any notes, even after I learned my range.

As a young teenager, one of my primary interests in church was watching people. Like everywhere, people came to church in all sizes, ages, and personality types, which kept me well entertained. As usual, during one of the long services, I turned around to see who sat behind me and there they were, the two spinster sisters, who were faithful members of the church and attended every service. I always thought they were somewhat humorous looking. They indeed were serious-minded and always wore plain, dark clothing. They also wore black bonnets with large bonnet pins secured on each side to keep them in place. They talked a lot with each other but were never very social with those around them.

The sermon and prayers must have been long that night, for I found myself merrily hatching a plan. At the end of the service, I decided to walk rapidly ahead of these two dear souls. Their bonnets were lying on the large, dark, wooden windowsill, as the ladies often removed their outdoor bonnets while in church. I remember quickly taking all four pins out of their bonnets, dropping them on the floor, and shoving them under the carpet with my foot. I then returned to our pew pretending I had forgotten something.

After returning to our pew, I now found myself behind the sisters as they went to the back of the church to get their coats and bonnets. I walked out slowly, watching to see what would happen, and feeling a little queasy inside. They kept looking and looking for their pins! They looked everywhere, well, everywhere but under the carpet! What a commotion I created. Soon, and probably way outside of their social comfort zone, they had others looking as well, but alas, to no avail. The pins were not found that day.

As I left the church, I couldn't help but laugh to myself because I had gotten away with this devilish act. Although I felt a twinge of guilt, I went away thinking, "Wow, no one saw me." It was not really like me to do such a foolish thing, especially to another person, with the constant threat of punishment of some kind always hanging over me, especially the threat of ending up in hell if I did something wrong. And even though I knew no one saw me, my mother's ever-present guiding voice rang loudly in my burning ears. "When you think no one is looking, God is always watching you." However, that night, I ignored her guidance despite the queasy feeling inside and my burning ears, and merrily completed my devilish subterfuge on the spinster sisters.

I'm certain "Spotty" was within me when I misplaced those bonnet pins.

Sometimes I think when a child grows up under rules that feel burdensome it is natural for them to test the waters and act out sooner or later. Believe me, to this day, I wish I could chat with those saintly sisters and apologize, perhaps even replace their missing bonnet pins.

# The House on Kissel Hill

*"Favorite people, favorite places, favorite memories of the past. These are the joys of a lifetime, these are the things that last."* ~Henry van Dyke

I have sweet memories of my Grandparents who lived on Kissel Hill Road, located near Lititz, Pennsylvania. As a child, their home was one of the world's best places to stay. If I was lucky enough, I stayed for a week at a time during the summers.

The big white house had coal black shutters, front and back porches with white pillars, and it lined up right alongside Kissel Hill road. Shady maple trees, English gardens, and beautiful velvety grass surrounded their house. The short dirt lane behind the house made its way to a red barn where my aunt parked her black, shiny 1946 Plymouth sedan.

This house on Kissel Hill was a haven where I felt truly loved and accepted. Feeling free as a bird, I loved exploring every room in the house. Could freedom bring so much happiness? My grandparents were like Zen listeners, always showing interest in my questions and the stories I shared. It is amazing what that kind of attention can do for a child.

One of my favorite rooms in their house was the back kitchen. As soon as my grandparents announced they were going for their afternoon nap, I would skip to the back room where I became anyone I wanted to be. Pretending to be a Mrs. Smith, I would step into an old pair of Grandma's black, high heeled shoes. I put on an apron and imitated walking around like Grandma. I cleaned and organized the shelves of canned food, swept the floor, and danced to the outside water pump to fill the silver sprinkling can so I could water the flowers. I would talk out loud to pretend people who stood there with me as we discussed the variety of flowers—"Did you ever smell the phlox?" I'd ask. "Oh yes, it's a summer gem and makes me smile," my pretend friend would reply.

My grandparents, Ephraim and Minnie, were like two peas in a pod and were gentle and loving people. Their house was simple but always very clean, a mirror reflection of their Swiss and German culture. "It doesn't cost anything to be clean," I would hear my Grandma say as she tidied the kitchen. She seemed to spend most of her time keeping things organized and tidy. Two of her favorite things to do were cooking in the kitchen and working in her English flower gardens, making sure no weeds appeared. My grandfather, on the other hand, loved to sit in one of the rockers on the front porch. He smoked his cherry cigars and watched the world go by. I would often sit by his side, talking non-stop, and he would listen intently.

Evenings were special because when my Aunt Blanche, who lived with them, came home from work, the house filled with even more energy and laughter. Grandma made sure that dinner was prepared on time, with a lovely table setting and delicious food. Like Mother's, her browned butter on the vegetables was to die for! The importance of time, routines, and rituals was evident as we sat down to eat. Someone would say grace, and then the food would be passed from left to right. The conversations centered around our activities, "So how was your day?" my aunt would ask. My grandma always smiled and said, "Another fun day, and Sandra was a big help."

After dinner, we would all help to clear the table, and wash and dry the dishes. They made me feel important as I participated. I couldn't wait to hear when my aunt suggested what we would do in the evening. Aunt Blanche was a single woman who worked full-time, lived with my grandparents, and was their caregiver until the time they died. She always had a bright idea, like, "Let's hop in the car and drive to the airport and watch the planes come in." Or "Let's go to the Lititz Park and feed the ducks." If it were raining, we'd stay at home and listen to the radio before we went to bed. We would often listen to classical music and just "be."

It's wonderful to remember the details of childhood adventures, especially the times when we were showered with the love and attention of our relatives. The house still stands along Kissel Hill road. I love to drive by and catch a glimpse of those beautiful childhood memories.

# Ahead of Her Time

*"You don't have to be a 'person of influence' to be influential.*
*In fact, the most influential people in my life are probably*
*not even aware of the things they've taught me."*
~Scott Adams

"Sandra," my Aunt Blanche said quietly, "must you dunk your doughnuts in your hot chocolate? We're in a public restaurant." I smiled, stopped dunking, and slowly finished the dry doughnut. After all, I was old enough to know better, but it had never occurred to me that this was not a proper thing to do. We dunked doughnuts, toast, and crackers in hot chocolate all the time at home.

If you met her, you might think my Aunt Blanche just stepped out of a P. Buckley Moss painting. She stood tall, conveying a commanding presence in her thick, black, high-heeled shoes. I thought to myself, *How does this lady always dress up, regardless of her activity, and maintain a hairstyle that never looks disturbed?* Oh, and there were her shiny black purses. She carried a different one almost every time I was with her. She greatly loved purses like most women do.

Aunt Blanche was the oldest child, born October 20, 1910, in Lancaster County, Pennsylvania. She had one sister—my dear mother—and two brothers. She drove a 1947 black Plymouth coupe. It had a blind, made of a lightweight vinyl material in the back window to keep the sun out. I would pull it down and latch it on a small hook below the window. How I would love to take one more ride, sit in the back seat, and pull the blind down just to hear the sound of the hook being latched, like I used to when I was a child.

Education was one of Aunt Blanche's priorities. She walked several miles each day to go to school beyond the eighth grade. She worked hard with her studies and was an honor student. She loved school, was surrounded by good friends, and enjoyed playing guard on her high school basketball team. I am fortunate to have inherited her letter "N" which she earned playing for Neffsville High School so many years ago. She lived with my grandparents and cared for them until they died. Later, she fell in love and married a widower when she was fifty years old.

My Aunt Blanche was soft-spoken, but her thoughtfulness and giving spirit sparkled like stars throughout her life. It was not unusual for her to take my grandparents or her girlfriends on trips to New England for sightseeing. You guessed it; we were always in for a treat at the next family reunion when she would show us her home movies. But our eye-rolling was all with great joy, for she was the first in the family to have a movie camera and a beautiful Zenith Radio. We did not have a TV, so Aunt Blanche's travelogue was big-time entertainment for us.

The added bonus while watching her silent movies was to hear the classical music she set up to play in the background. I credit her for introducing me to all kinds of music and to an expansive world that existed outside of Lancaster County, Pennsylvania.

Photography, reading, and traveling were her passions. As a child, I can still remember asking, "Aunt Blanche, may I carry your camera case while you take movies?" She would smile and drape the strap over my shoulder. I proudly followed her around like a young filly in training.

Watching some of her old movie tapes today, which are now on DVDs, reconnects me with her positive energy.

"So, Mother," I asked one day, "why didn't Aunt Blanche get married when she was younger?" My mother smiled and replied, "Well, the way I see it, she was popular with the boys and she did date. In fact, one of her suitors was auspicious, but she was very independent and said no. She could have married, but she chose to take care of your grandparents, work, and travel."

One day when my aunt was visiting us on the farm, she asked, "Sandra, how would you like to come with me to New York City the next time I go on business?" I was as excited as a playful kitten and said, "Yes, I would love to go along!" The details of that trip are another story, but I can share now that I learned quickly that New York City was not at all the same as Lancaster City, Pennsylvania.

After getting off of the bus in New York City, I had to use the restroom, and I gleefully said, "Oh Aunt Blanche, there is a place to go down to the bathroom, right across the street." She started giggling and said, "No Sandra, that goes down to the subway." But in Lancaster, there was a stairway along the street that led down to the public restrooms. She said, "Things are different here." I was only fourteen, and it was obvious that I had lived a sheltered life. As she held my hand on the way to the restroom at the back of an exclusive textile establishment, she said, "This is New York City, a place you will never forget."

My aunt had twelve nieces and nephews, and she made it a priority to do something special with each of us. Whenever it was my turn, she treated me as though I were the only person in the universe. She took a genuine interest in us and asked questions like, "How is school going?" "Do you keep up with your homework?" "Do you have good friends?"

One day, she gently took my hand and examined my nails. "Sandra," she asked, "do you clean your nails every day?" I sheepishly replied, "Usually." She expounded on how important it was as a teenager, to take good care of my hygiene. My mother taught us good manners, but it seemed that my aunt always took that two-steps further.

I now realize that my aunt's presence woke me up from my ordinary life. I learned how important it is to have an education, and that girls can do anything they set their minds to. I learned to love photography, art, classical music, reading, and travel. Maybe that is why, in college, I majored in art education. I learned that caring for our parents the best way we know how is essential. But mostly, I learned how she lived life to the fullest, and she did it her way, without regrets.

In my mind, Aunt Blanche was a woman ahead of her time. She had no idea how closely I watched her under my mental microscope, intrigued with how she made powerful choices. Her example of gratitude and keeping her faith melted into my being like starlight, illuminating my whole worldview.

My nails might not always be clean enough to meet her specifications, but for sure, you'll never catch me in public, dunking doughnuts in my hot chocolate, no matter how dry they are. Come into my kitchen, though, and when I tell you to go ahead and dunk your doughnut, you might discover that I can make powerful choices too.

## PART TWO

# School Years

# The Joy of Handwriting

*"Handwriting is a spiritual designing, even though it appears by means of a material instrument."* ~Euclid

"Okay class," the teacher said, "let's begin with using our hands, motioning in the air." Up down, up down, our hands would go, in rhythm, straight, sometimes slanted, practicing those letters from the bottom of the line to the top, yes in the air, *A, B, C.* "Now that we are ready," Mrs. Eyster said, "please take out your penmanship books, and we will practice writing." We made straight strokes, slanted strokes, and those round slanted circles over and over. Then letter-by-letter we practiced writing the alphabet. It felt like we were dancing across the paper. I fell in love with learning to write in cursive, and to this day I love the motion of my pen as it glides over the paper. There was something about the appearance of a handwritten page that brought me joy. Soon we were learning to write notes in cursive to our parents, grandparents, and friends. Connecting those letters in cursive became a special way to communicate with family and friends.

The teacher often asked us to write a poem or a story in cursive. We took pride in every letter and made sure it was properly placed on the specially lined paper. We would practice and fill many pages with penmanship, trying to capture the beauty of cursive handwriting. The more I wrote in cursive, the less I enjoyed printing, and to this day I don't feel I can print very well. That being said, it isn't even necessary.

Handwriting has evolved throughout history in different ways. Learning to write in cursive was a requirement during my elementary years in the 1950s. It was a true achievement and an art form. I earned a certificate from The Peterson System of Directed Handwriting for the Public Schools stating that I had attained a satisfactory degree of skill in handwriting. It makes me smile, and that is why I still have the certificate. I continued to enjoy writing in cursive throughout my elementary years.

The exercise of learning to write in cursive was priceless in so many ways, not only for the sense of achievement in learning something "grown-up," but also for the beauty of it. Each person's handwriting is a little different, like a fingerprint and a reflection of their individuality. It makes receiving a handwritten letter extra special. I will always enjoy handwriting. I will continue to enjoy writing notes even though these days, I also use all kinds of technology along with everyone else. "Up down, up down," my hand will go even if it is just for the pure enjoyment of seeing the end result on paper. The meaning of the word "cursive," is a style of writing, in which all the letters in a word are connected. Cursive comes from the Latin word "currere," meaning "to run." And that is what I did. I ran with my pen and pencil and have loved the exercise ever since.

# Mrs. Eyster

*"A good teacher can inspire hope, ignite the imagination, and instill a love of learning."* -Brad Henry

When I skipped home from school, the priority was to do my chores before doing homework. Well, unless I blended both jobs. I usually went right to the chicken house, taking a piece of chalk, a pencil, paper, and of course, the egg basket. As soon as I entered the chicken house, I became Mrs. Eyster. I found it humorous that, as soon as the chickens saw me, they stopped cackling just like the students did at school when Mrs. Eyster appeared. I would greet them and explain, just like Mrs. Eyster, that it was time to collect their homework.

I went from nest to nest collecting eggs, and said, "Good Jane, good Susan," and when I came to an empty nest I would look right at the "student" and ask why she didn't have her homework finished. The hen would look at me with her head tilted to the side, as if to say, "Are you serious?"

After gathering the eggs and making sure I had them counted correctly, I was ready to review math, spelling words, and geography. I remember asking my "cackling students" the capitals of the states, and with my chalk, I wrote the answers on the barn wall. There was always one chicken that would cackle louder than the others, and I would point to that one for the answer. When I raised my voice with glee, most of the cackling would stop, and they would look at me for a few seconds. This daily routine became more and more intriguing because I was learning the behavior of chickens. I also had fun completing my homework.

My school was only three blocks from home, an easy walk. I remember the rugged set of steps to the main entrance led to two small, enclosed closets on each side of the entryway. Inside of each closet, there was a row of black metal hooks for students to hang our coats and hats on.

Arranged across the main room with its creaking, wooden floors, there were eight rows of desks, one for each grade. A large, coal, potbelly stove stood near the center of the room and was regularly used during the winter. The students often gathered around the stove to warm up. The smell of wet gloves and hats spread on the floor to dry often lingered in the room. A tattered brown wooden desk sat at the front of the room near the long blackboard that covered the wall, similar to what you can see in one of Norman Rockwell's schoolroom paintings.

Many teachers were hired to teach at this rural school. During my first year, it was evident the administration had a difficult time finding an excellent teacher who would be willing to stay for the entire year. During first grade, I had three different teachers who were somewhat eccentric, and I wonder to this day if they were properly certified to teach.

In my second year, the school district hired Mrs. Eyster, a lovely older lady. She had gray hair, stood 5-feet tall, was kind of plump, and wore mostly A-line dresses. I can still hear her walking around the room, wearing her black, medium-height heels and striding like she was on a mission. I was intrigued by her mannerisms and watched her intently. When she came to my desk to help me with a problem, I can still hear the funny sound she made while she waited for an answer. It was between a hiccup and clearing her throat.

Having her as a teacher improved things at this little school. She had high expectations, was very strict, and if anyone ever got out of line, she made sure she used one of her punishment options.

For example, there was Thomas, a towering eighth grader who loved to show off his muscles. He seemed to enjoy wasting time when he should have been doing his assignments. One time he threw something across the room and that upset Mrs. Eyster. She asked him to come to the front of the room and hold out his hands. He obediently marched up the aisle as she took a ruler from her desk and when he got to her, she slapped the palms of his hands ten times. I almost got sick to my stomach because I had never seen this kind of punishment before. Thomas just stood there and grinned

100

the whole time while she administered the punishment, though I'm sure it made his hands sore. To this day I'm wondering if the joke was on Mrs. Eyster. He was one tough cookie.

During my first three years, there were only three of us in my grade, Eddie, May, and myself. May was known to be a slow student. Maybe it was because she came from a family of nine sisters and lacked attention! Eddie was sharp as a tack, and I enjoyed competing with him. Sometimes Mrs. Eyster would ask the eighth graders to help us, perhaps by listening to us read from the *Dick and Jane* books or by guiding us in math. I paid close attention to how she meandered around the room, managing to effectively teach eight different grades. I thought, *Someday I want to be a teacher just like her.*

She was an expert at teaching cackling students, and I enjoyed adopting some of her skills in my pretend world.

The little, red brick, one-room schoolhouse no longer exists in Starview. However, the memories of those first three years in grade school continue to glow.

Those were the days, when parents and teachers supported each other. I remember when my mother invited Mrs. Eyster to our house for dinner. The respect between them was evident. During my 50s, I returned to the farm in Starview to see if my writing was still on the barn wall. Sure enough, to my delight, I could see a faint imprint of many of the words I had written for my well educated chickens.

# Music with Mrs. Moore

*"To escape fear, you have to go through it, not around."*
~Richie Norton

Music class with Mrs. Moore in second grade was something I dreaded. It was here I was forced to face my biggest childhood fears. I was a shy child and often acted like a scared pup. Although I loved music, performing in front of the class terrified me.

I was fascinated by Mrs. Moore's passion for music. She played the piano with gusto and sang like a lark. She taught music to all the students in our one-room schoolhouse, all at the same time, a feat that would seem almost impossible. But not for Mrs. Moore; she walked with confidence and spoke with authority.

At home, I imitated playing the piano like Mrs. Moore. I would play using my whole body, just like my teacher did, swaying back and forth over the keys. My mom would chuckle and say, "Keep practicing." Music was fun and comfortable at home—at school, it was a different story.

As soon as Mrs. Moore opened the wooden doors and came into the room, I would become anxious and nervous. As she moved to the front of the room, I got the jitters, anticipating what would happen next. My body would wobble like Jell-O even before she began teaching.

Mrs. Moore used her teaching skills with all eight grades in a creative fashion. She would divide us into three groups according to our grade levels: first through fourth, fifth and sixth, seventh and eighth. At the beginning of each class, she gave out individual assignments incorporating different instruments, and the challenge began. We used instruments like the triangle, the wood blocks, maracas, and tambourines to name a few.

The group that I was in had to practice using the percussion instruments. Each week, we were asked to choose a different instrument. Mrs. Moore's goal was to have each student participate in every activity and learn how to play each instrument. The collision of sounds must have been heard throughout the neighborhood, Sam banging on the drum while Susan was making a ruckus on the flute.

It was fine until the time came when she asked us to line up like soldiers between the rows of desks. My heart sank as the organization of us players began. She chose someone to be the leader, and we had to march up and down each row while she played the piano and we played our instruments. To me, this was dreadful, and I wanted to shrink inside my own skin. I was way outside of my comfort zone.

This is where the challenge began for me. I did not feel comfortable if I was called upon. I cooperated, but where was Mrs. Moore's empathy? She just moved forward ignoring tears or hurt feelings. I always gave her credit for being a good teacher, but she lacked a few skills in the caring department.

I realize those were my fears I carried with me, not hers. I had a sheltered home life, and this made it very difficult for me to feel free-spirited. Inwardly, I wanted to be confident, but many times I had problems openly revealing that side of myself.

When we marched past the seventh and eighth graders, some of the boys were notorious for teasing me and pulling my pigtails. It was worse when she asked me to be the leader; the boys teased me even more.

As soon as Mrs. Moore saw me crying, she would say, "Sandra, you may go sit at your desk." I don't know if she was showing me kindness or if this just made it worse. As I sat waiting for my group to finish their march, I felt acutely alone in my embarrassment.

After many years, I now realize Mrs. Moore was an excellent teacher who wanted us to learn and appreciate music. Maybe she was a little rough around the edges, but by the end of the year, I eventually became more comfortable. It took facing my fears over and over again, going through them, to overcome them. Though I still had a long way to go, with each march down the rows, I became a bit more confident and more comfortable.

From Mrs. Moore I learned to never give up, and to keep practicing activities outside of my comfort zone.

# Eddie, May, and I

*"Sometimes you will never know the value of something until it becomes a memory."* ~Dr. Seuss

If you were lucky enough to go to a one-room schoolhouse, you were lucky enough. I wasn't always eager to share that I went to a one-room schoolhouse, but now realize it was one of the best experiences I had in life. Growing older often brings new insights and appreciation. I have vivid memories of how the teachers, parents, and students worked so harmoniously together.

Our school had eight straight rows of wooden desks, each with its own inkwell and pencil holder. The desks and seats had fancy black metal legs and were screwed to the floor, keeping them in place. This was a great help for the teacher to keep us neatly lined up. The seats folded up and down and I thought it was the neatest thing to maneuver, and for some reason I loved the sound, *ker-plunk, ker-plunk.*

All eight grades were often divided into smaller, mixed groups of students. Sometimes the teacher would announce, "Today I would like the eighth graders to come up front to the large table and help the fifth graders with math, while I teach the other groups."

We were a trio in first, second, and third grades, Eddie, May, and I. We each sat at our small individual wooden desks, arranged in a row behind each other. I remember the empty inkwells that we didn't use and the long groove at the top of my desk where I loved placing my new pencils. I enjoyed putting my books on top of the desk and kept everything else organized inside the cubbyhole within the desk. We were the only three in the same grade so we stuck together like glue.

Eddie was cute, smart as a whip, and short like me. He was quiet, with a kindhearted personality. The other students often teased us, saying that he was my boyfriend. "Oh Sandra," they said, "you two look so adorable beside each other." We just smiled and then went on our way. I was an overachiever, and worked hard to do well in school. Reading, spelling, and geography were my favorite subjects, but please, not math. May, who was tall as a corn stalk, struggled with all of her lessons, so much so, that she had to repeat the third grade. She came from a large family of nine sisters, and was the youngest, shy as a frightened kitten. Why she struggled so much with her studies, I don't know. I don't think it was for lack of parental attention; she certainly reflected abundant, loving, parental attention in the looks department. While I wore the simple, print dresses Mother made me, May was always dressed in frills and lace and shiny shoes, usually with fancy white socks.

Since we were all in one room, it was intimidating sometimes, being with the older students. If anyone made a mistake or got in trouble, everyone could hear. As you can imagine, the teacher had to have eyes in the back of her head and be alert at all times. During my first three years, the district had a difficult time getting a full-time teacher, and I remember one year having a male teacher who seemed to be there just to fill the chair at the desk. I don't remember learning much from him, or maybe I learned how *not* to be a teacher!

Mr. Johnson was a tall and lanky man, and often wore wrinkly shirts. I don't remember him standing in front of the class very often. He sat at his desk mostly giving out assignments. He said, "First, second, and third grades, you will have reading and then complete the assignment in your workbook. Fourth, fifth, and sixth grades work on your math. Seventh and eighth grades you will have a geography test." I don't remember him actually teaching, so if someone had a question, he would make sure one of the students helped. Also when he was there, our recesses lasted much longer than usual, which of course, we didn't mind at all. He blew his nose all the time, honking like a goose, and instead of putting his tissues in the trash he stored them in the bottom drawer of his huge clunky desk. Thank goodness he was only there for half of the year.

Being in a small class was a real advantage because we received a lot of help if needed and sometimes the older students doubled up to read and work together with writing exercises. We, the trio, did our best to learn and were cooperative students. For reading we went up front and sat on a long bench where we had to read out loud. Either the teacher or an older student listened while we read.

For me, going to school was the beginning of learning how to be in two very different worlds—my strict and conservative home life, vs. my public-school life. Religion played a large part in my life at home and there were often discussions around the dinner table about whether or not I should dance around the maypole, celebrate Halloween, or even pledge allegiance to the flag at school. *What harm was there in dancing around the maypole or dressing in costume and eating yummy candy?* I wondered. Since I was so young, my parents, sometimes reluctantly, allowed me to participate in some of the activities at school with the rest of the students.

Paddling was a common punishment in schools as well as in homes during that era. If I got punished at school, for goofing off or talking back to the teacher, I usually got punished at home too. It depended on your parents. Paddling and having to sit on a stool with a dunce hat on in front of everyone were the two most dreaded experiences. At our school we had a coal shed and I can remember the teacher telling a student to go to the shed and we knew what was next. We could not always hear the crack of the whip, but we could hear the cry. It took a long time for many states to ban corporal punishment. It was finally banned in Pennsylvania in 2009.

The students, teachers, and community were like one big family supporting each other. Mother would say from time to time, "Sandra, here is a note for your teacher, I'm inviting her to come for dinner next week." I actually looked forward to her visits. Sitting at the dinner table with my teacher and family was like a scene out of the *Little House on the Prairie* TV series. We had interesting conversations during those times because we discussed current events, like what was happening in the Korean war and the latest on the polio vaccine, which had recently been introduced. For me these were much more interesting topics than our usual discussion of chores! There were many positive experiences at school, compared to the strict rules of home life.

As I reflect on this period of my life, I can still hear the squeaky sound of the wooden floors, I can still smell the coal burning in the potbelly stove, taste the delicious lunches mother made, and see a room filled with lovely children and one of my favorite teachers.

I am sure the three of us were gems as a trio, Eddie, May, and I. We made good music, learned a lot together, and made many joyful memories. We were put together for a reason, if only to walk side-by-side helping each other during those three memorable years.

# Shenanigans with Catherine

*"A friend is one of the nicest things you can have and one of the best things you can be." ~*Douglas Pagels

I am convinced that people come into our lives for a reason. And when they do, how many of us stay connected for life? I met Catherine in fourth grade, and we stayed in touch all through life.

Catherine was the friend I always counted on. Her quiet personality was calming for me since I was the opposite. What we had in common was strict parents, but different religions. My family was Mennonite and hers was Lutheran.

No subject was off limits between the two of us when we got together and started talking. One day she said to me, "You know Sandra, I don't think my mom likes me." I said, "What makes you think that?" "Well," she said, "she criticizes the way I look, the way I walk. I can't seem to please her." "Well," I said, "my dad is the same way, and I don't like it either." We could relate to each other's challenges. "Catherine, can you help me with math?" "Sure," she'd say, "and you can help me with spelling." I called her my math expert as she helped me solve those dang long division problems.

During my fourth-grade year, students were bussed from their small communities, after the one-room schoolhouses closed and new schools were built. We were bussed to a building in a larger town, Mt. Wolf, a few minutes away from where we lived.

Our fourth-grade class took place in a large room with high ceilings above a store in an old building. There were three floors, and we were on the second floor. The dark brown wood trim on the doorway and the worn hardwood floors made the whole room look dim. With only a few windows across the front of the building, just a glimpse of sunlight reached our room. A few drab looking bulletin boards hung along one wall beside a worn black chalkboard. This was not an inviting room for anyone, especially children.

Our teacher, Mrs. Fields, a pleasant and kind-hearted woman with salt and pepper hair, knew how to run her class. "Good morning class," she always greeted us in her cheerful voice. "It's time to pledge allegiance to the flag and sing 'America The Beautiful.'" We looked like little soldiers lined up behind our desks as we almost shouted the pledge and sang as loud as we could.

Mrs. Fields had a system for everything! For example, when we had to use the bathroom, which was on the third floor, she had, hanging near the door, a wooden leaf that was painted green on one side and red on the other. When someone went to the bathroom, they turned the leaf red, which meant no one else was allowed to go to the third floor during that time. And when they returned, they'd turn the leaf back to green.

Catherine and I had other ideas. We were always afraid to go to the bathroom alone, especially when we heard there was a stranger in the area trying to pick up children. We had a plan.

"Sandra," she whispered one day, "are you ready for our get-away?" I sat there giggling inside, trying not to let the teacher hear me. "Yes," I said, "you go first."

When one of us had to go to the bathroom, we pretended to forget to turn the leaf red before we went up the long flight of stairs. That, of course, gave the other person freedom to go up the stairs a little later. We also made sure we each put a ruler inside our blouse so we'd be armed, just in case we encountered some stranger on the third floor. We'd get to the top of the long stairway and wait for each other.

We stood there like two birds meeting on a branch, whispering and laughing. "I'm sure glad our plan is working so far," I told Catherine.

While one of us was in the bathroom, the other would keep watch for any stranger, ruler at the ready. Before we returned, we made our rounds, peeking into dark closets and into the different rooms. We were on the lookout for the man who was stalking children, though, thank goodness, we never encountered him. It was creepy being on the third floor. The dark rooms were used for storage, and they smelled disgustingly musty.

"Catherine," I said, "I just saw a mouse run across the room, let's get out of here!" Our nervousness made us giggle.

We were always relieved to return to the classroom. One of us would go back down and enter the room, and the other one waited for a few minutes until we felt it was safe to return without the teacher seeing us. I don't remember how many times we implemented this grand plan, but it seemed to work. Did the teacher ever notice? We'll never know, but I have my suspicions.

At recess, we played on the rough, pebbled alley behind the school or on a cement driveway connected to the building. There was no grass on the playground so we were limited as to what we could do. Some of our favorite activities were playing tag, hide and seek, or Freddie would yell, "I'm playing marbles on the ground, anyone joining me?" And the girls, especially, loved jump rope, so Mary, Catherine, and I would jump and shout, "Down the Mississippi! Where the steamboats go! Some go fast! Some go slow! Down the Mississippi! Where the steamboats go! PUSH!" Jumper exits, new jumper enters.

When it rained during recess, we were allowed to go down to the store on the first floor. On one particular day, I followed Catherine to the store as usual. We walked up and down the aisles and loved looking at the candy in the bins.

"What are you planning to buy today, Catherine?" I asked. "I'm not sure," she said, "maybe bubble gum." These bins were the size of large crates, without lids, higher than our waist, filled to the brim with candy. "Catherine," I said, "we could actually hide in these bins underneath the candy if we had to." I'm sure the store-owner could hear us giggling.

Catherine usually had money to buy candy. Whenever she purchased some, she would share with me. That day as I was watching her, I saw her take a few pieces of candy, and she stuck them straight into her pocket. I was shocked! I went up to her and quietly, but very forthrightly, said, "Catherine, don't you know that is stealing?" She looked at me and said, "Sandra, do you think they will ever miss it, having all these bins full of candy?" I thought, of course not, so I too, took a few pieces and put them in my pocket feeling very shaky inside. This was the first and last time I remember stealing. To this day, I always regretted participating. I wanted to return to the owner and apologize later. I never did, but I hope I was forgiven by the Almighty!

We were both churchgoers, and I didn't understand why her religion was less strict and she could steal without feeling bad. She seemed to chalk it up as a fun happening. Catherine asked, "What makes you think someone saw us?" "Well," I said, "my mother always taught me that God sees everything we do." "Well, of course, God saw us," she replied, "but if no one else did we'll be fine." I didn't understand her thinking, but I realize now how I took everything literally from what I was taught at home, and I was taught that ours was not a forgiving God. In those days no cameras were hanging anywhere. The owner was responsible for being on the lookout for thieves. I'm sure we looked too innocent to be suspects. Thankfully neither of us became criminals.

Later in life we would often sit and reminisce about the times we acted out of character and got away with nonsense. We laughed and laughed like we did in fourth grade. Those memories are priceless, and today I miss Catherine more than she knows. My mother often reminded me, "If you go through life having one loyal friend, you are blessed." Shenanigans or not, she was a real friend. She made life look so easy, going with the flow and knowing how to laugh. Her personal faith was visible, just different in the way she showed it. I remember telling her one time, "I'd like to be a Lutheran," and we giggled again.

Catherine and I stayed in close contact until she died in 2014. Occasionally I find myself acting a little out of character, looking up to Heaven and wondering if she and her forgiving God are giggling with me. Catherine brought humor to our adventures and even though we are apart, I still laugh out loud sometimes, remembering them. Her spirit is as close as my shadow, glowing with happy memories. After she died, I found myself picking up pennies on the ground and saving them like she did. It was those simple things she did that made me smile.

Catherine's presence in my life showed me what a true friend is, supportive and caring regardless of our differences. She helped me to lighten up when times were dark and gloomy. She showed me what contentment means by being authentic. Her priorities were not centered around having a lot of things, but instead, she invested in friendships. I was one of the fortunate recipients and will always be grateful.

# The 23<sup>rd</sup> Psalm

*"Too often we underestimate the power of a touch, a smile,
a kind word, a listening ear, an honest compliment, or the
smallest act of caring, all of which have the potential to
turn a life around."* -Leo Buscaglia

From the time I began to read, I had to memorize verses from the Bible, and at church I earned red tickets, as did the other children, when we recited them correctly. After we accumulated a certain number of tickets, we each got to choose a prize. We could pick something from the basket, like a plastic cross, an angel that glowed in the dark, or a bookmarker with pictures from the Bible.

New schools were still under construction as I entered fifth grade. So I now took a different bus to yet another new school, located in Manchester, Pennsylvania, a few minutes from our house. Our fifth grade class was held on the second floor of a fire hall. You guessed it, sirens would go off any time of the day, and it was certainly alarming.

I didn't like this school or my teacher. Mrs. Hiller was somewhat classy looking, always had her white hair in place, but she was slow to share her smiles. She was strict, requiring us to use good manners and show respect for others. What bothered me was that I felt that she picked on me too often and embarrassed me in front of my classmates. "Sandra, stop talking." "Sandra, sit along the wall by yourself to work on your math problems." "Sandra, stay in for recess today." "Not again," I mumbled to myself, "why doesn't she pick on someone else?" She frightened me so much that when I was called on, the words would freeze in my mouth. I wanted to participate like everyone else, but I struggled. I needed "Surely goodness and mercy"!

I loved to talk with my friends and I must admit, I chatted too much when I should have been focusing on my work. The teacher had every right to move me further away from my friends, even though I made a point to talk and continued to get into more trouble over and over again. I wasn't a troublemaker, just a chatterbox.

The highlight for me was recess time. I loved jumping rope and playing hide and seek. I especially enjoyed having recess during October. It was the time of the apple harvest!

There was a dear lady who lived next to the fire hall. She was short, friendly, and usually wore an apron. We never knew when she would come out of her house, but when she appeared, we all got excited.

In October, she often came out of her home with a wheelbarrow of candy apples arranged on wax paper. Like ants, we all got in a straight line and waited for our turn. We could pay her ten cents for a candy apple or, if we recited the 23rd Psalm, "The Lord is my shepherd; I shall not want..." We would get a free candy apple! Many could not recite the 23rd Psalm, so they asked to borrow money from others. This was one time I was happy that I had to memorize Bible verses in church! Psalm 23 was one of my favorite passages, so it was easy to recite.

The memory of the lady bringing us candy apples in a wheelbarrow and asking us to recite the 23rd Psalm almost seems surreal. What was the relevance for a fifth grader to recite these verses? A free candy apple, yes, and to meet an earth angel who brought the verses to light. She was like a shepherd looking over her flock, sharing her delicious apples and making our "cup runneth over with joy."

# First-Time Experiences

*"Experience is one thing you can't get for nothing."*
~Oscar Wilde

The 6$^{th}$ grade, for me, brought the joys of many first-time experiences, including attendance at another new school in York Haven, just ten minutes from home. Many cars filled the small parking lot, and a playground with maple trees surrounded the school.

During recess, my friend Catherine and I hung out on the playground to talk. One day, she said, "Go look at Marsha's hair." Slowly I snuck up behind Marsha to get a closer look. I saw that her head was crawling with lice. One of the students told the teacher and after she examined Marsha's head, she sent her to the nurse. At the end of the day a note was sent home for our parents to keep watch. If lice were detected, instructions were provided for what kind of products to use to wash with. Fortunately, I don't remember ever having them, but I still itch as I remember seeing Marsha's scalp in motion. It was the first time I ever saw lice, and I hoped the last.

Whenever it rained, we had to stay inside for recess and play. I remember the time there was a lot of laughter and commotion as some of the girls took turns going inside a closet in the back of the room, as though there were something secretive going on. Sure enough, some of the girls had gotten their first bra and were letting the rest of us see. I remember going home that day in tears, saying, "Mother, I want a bra." She said, "Oh Sandra, there is no hurry, and I don't think you need one yet." I cried for a long time, wanting to be like the others. A few days later, Mother said she had something for me. She had made my first bra out of silk material without any padding. I wasn't thrilled, but thanked her and saved the day by puffing out those flat little cups with tissues. I was only brave enough to show my best girlfriend.

My 6ᵗʰ-grade teacher was Mrs. Zeigler, who loved teaching, and enjoyed bringing out the best in her students. We felt her kindness and joy each day, as we entered her classroom. She always greeted us with a smile and seemed happy to see us. I loved the spelling bees on Fridays and had the pleasure of winning one of those for the first time in 6ᵗʰ grade. Winning was a delightful highlight for me in Mrs. Zeigler's class. She gave me a book called *Heidi*, for winning the spelling bee and although the cover is faded, it still stands on my bookshelf these many years later.

My mother bought me a bubblegum pink plastic wallet to take to school that year. It was my first wallet, and I treasured using it daily. My heart sank the day I went looking for my lunch money, and I couldn't find my wallet. In tears, I told my teacher, and she said she and the staff would look for it.

The next day Mrs. Zeigler said, "Sandra, the janitor, Mr. Bumps, found your wallet. He said he discovered it in one of the car fenders in the parking lot." I don't remember if my money was still in it, but I sure was happy to have my pink wallet returned.

Mr. Bumps, forty-something, was the first person I met who was totally deaf and could not talk. He was the kindest man, with a contagious smile, and he enjoyed teaching us sign language. I liked when he sat with us during lunchtime and showed us how to sign. He beamed when we signed correctly. We were eager to learn so we could communicate with him better. He was known to be a hard worker, treated the students with respect, and was loved by everyone.

My first-time experiences in 6ᵗʰ grade did not make headline news, but they made an impression on me forever.

# Wanting to Fit In!

*"Every struggle in your life has shaped you into the person you are today. Be thankful for the hard times, they can only make you stronger."* ~Keanu Reeves

From the 7th to 12th grades, I found myself challenged by much more than just adolescence, as I became acutely aware of the difference between the two worlds I inhabited. One was the world of public school, where I found myself surrounded by others who did not have to conform to the strictures of my other world, the world of our plain Mennonite church that required us to behave in certain ways, and to conform to a dress code that was clearly different from those who were not members.

I had mostly good teachers at school. I enjoyed going, but had to work hard with my studies, and looking back, it wasn't fun trying to be a perfectionist. Part of my salvation was being surrounded by wonderful friends who were kind-hearted, helpful, and loved to laugh. You need that especially when you live in two worlds.

One of my biggest challenges came when I joined the plain Mennonite church where my parents were members. Generally, Mennonite parents bring their young children to church when they go, but it's not until the children get older that they are offered the opportunity to join formally.

I was encouraged to become a Christian and join the church the summer before I started 7th grade, and I decided to join, but I was so young that my decision came mostly out of fear, rather than devotion. I remember standing in the kitchen, opening the refrigerator door, while my mother was at the sink working. I softly said, "Mother, I would like to become a Christian." She said, "Wonderful Sandra, we'll make sure to tell the pastor and then talk about formally joining the church." Right then and there I wanted to run in another direction. I had no problem becoming a Christian, but I was afraid of joining this ultraconservative church because I knew that my behavior and dress would then make me visibly different from those who were not members of the church. At this time in my life, when I wanted so much to fit in, this felt like a huge challenge. Through membership, I would experience a sense of belonging, having other Mennonite friends, but also the sense of being different, the more I became exposed to the outside world as I grew older.

Most young people were encouraged to become Christian and join the church at the onset of adolescence. Teenagers want to fit in, to be a part of a group, and I was no exception. I decided if I joined the church, I could fit in with my peers at church, but I had no idea how I'd feel after I joined and what it would be like to go to a public school, the other world, where contrast was unavoidable.

The requirements and expectations felt like a massive millstone around my neck. I did not feel comfortable in the way I had to dress and the way I was expected to look. For example, I always had to hide my beautiful long hair and put it up in a bun like an elderly person. Then I had to put a prayer covering on top of that bun. Talk about feeling top heavy. The white covering did not really cover my head or all of my long hair. I began questioning silently why it was necessary, because I felt I could pray just as well with or without it. I'm convinced that is true for me today. The men who held positions of leadership in this church took their responsibilities very seriously, and as a member, I was expected to conform to the rules even if I didn't understand them or agree with them. I felt that many of the rules made women look odd and peculiar, while the men seemed to look mostly ordinary. This was a challenge I struggled to make sense of.

An example of my quandary was one day at high school when I was in study hall. I sat beside a senior, and I was a freshman. He looked at the prayer covering on my head and asked, "Sandra, why do you wear that on your head?" I said, "I don't know, ask my mother." We both kind of chuckled. I was so embarrassed, so frightened inside because I knew I did not do these things from my heart; I did them out of a sense of duty, and a part of me wished I didn't have to, sitting beside that senior boy that day.

I wore "plain" dresses mostly just for church. Fortunately, I did not have to wear them to school after middle school, because I begged my way out of it in order to avoid drawing attention to myself among the other students. Plain dress requires wearing a cape on top of your dress, and the cape goes from your shoulders to your waste. It was worn to show modesty and avoid showing the shape of your bust. I looked around at the other women at church and noticed that regardless of the modest lines of the capes, they were clearly different sizes. Modesty might just be in the eye of the beholder, because you could not hide those larger sizes!

Joining a church that I didn't fully understand as a teenager felt awkward from the beginning. I struggled with the dogma, trying to make sense of rules that seemed inconsistent or contradictory. I wondered if God would expect strict adherence to such a long list of requirements. Whether I was in school or church, I had to make decisions centered on the church rules, which even covered whether or not I was allowed to part my hair in the middle or on the side. One time I was getting ready for Bible school and decided to part my hair on the right side. My thought was, if it were on the right side, it would be acceptable. As I was leaving the house, my dad noticed and he said, "Sandra, you are not allowed to go to church with your hair parted on the right." It was one of the first times I pushed against these boundaries and said, "Well then, I will not go to church." I was amazed that my parents went ahead without me, and to this day, I wonder who suffered the most, my parents forging ahead without my presence, or me feeling left behind simply because I had parted my hair on the side. My father was so concerned that his family appeared to be following every rule to the T that sometimes the rules felt more important than we did!

As for dating, like many people who are devoted to their faiths, we were discouraged from having boyfriends who were not church members of our denomination. I was not allowed to date until I was sixteen. And even then there were rules around who I could spend time with—no Catholics, Lutherans, Presbyterians, or people of a different faith. If I had crushes on guys at school, which I did, I had to keep them a secret. In fact, I liked a guy for a few months in secret, and as he caught on, we became close friends. His locker was near mine, and one day he gave me a box of valentine candy. I remember feeling very nervous and knew I could not take the candy home, so I kept it in my locker, sharing the candy with my friends. Inwardly I would have loved to take it home to share, but there were many lines I was afraid to cross. Yes, those rules brought anguish over many things that my school friends never had to consider, and I keenly felt the challenges.

I loved gym class, and I was allowed to participate in most activities but unfortunately, not dancing. I was always in charge of the record player for that activity, which made me feel isolated and perplexed. But what topped it off was wearing a prayer covering with a gym suit. Seriously, I might as well have been wearing a sign that said "Look at me, I'm different!" Inside I felt flustered and annoyed because I wanted to blend in with the others. It's amazing the strength you can build within yourself with those kinds of experiences. By the time I was a junior, I had started leaving my covering in the locker during gym class because there was no way I wanted it to fly off while tumbling on the gymnastics mat. It felt empowering to make that choice even though the guilt nearly choked me. I just wanted to fit in!

I always looked forward to the school plays and longed to participate. "No," my parents said, "that activity is too showy." The good news came when it was time to try out for the chorus. I knew the chorus was acceptable and I always made it. I remember clearly standing at the piano with the music teacher as she listened to my voice going up and down the scales. She said, "Sandra you will sing alto, but to be sure, let's do this again, and please sing a little louder." I was tested again, and had to force myself to project my voice, probably subconsciously trying not to be too showy.

It was tough trying to live in these two conflicting worlds. I enjoyed my school and church friends. I was more comfortable with my church friends but always wanted to be more like my school friends. There was that constant feeling of conflict like I was caught in a web and couldn't get free. There were about 1,000 students in my school from 7th to 12th grade, with only three plain Mennonites in the whole school. To some degree, I know what being part of a minority feels like and now wonder about one of my classmates. How must he have felt being the only black student in our class and in the whole school?

What I learned through those teenage years was that some plain Mennonite parents were not nearly as strict as mine. I always envied my girlfriends who were allowed to buy purses and shoes with a little glitz, or who had more freedoms. I did the best I could, but it wasn't easy. I experienced equal strictness both at church and at home.

My face turned embarrassing shades of red many times while trying to be a plain Mennonite. For some, it is a comforting and uplifting lifestyle, most especially if they choose it because they want to, not because they have to, or because they are afraid. I did not feel free to say, "No I do not want to join this church." I was very young and terrified of going to the fiery furnace if I didn't join.

The saying, "a cat has nine lives" reminds me that I have also experienced several. No, I did not have a near encounter with death, but I endured years of struggle and conflict with each new chapter of growth and increased exposure to the outside world. I survived it. Time and experience have taught me that it's not a religion's dogma that is most important. What's important is each person's true connection to the Divine power that is at work in the universe and within each one of us.

# Stepping into a New Era

*"There are far better things ahead than any we leave behind."*
~C.S. Lewis

*Another change!* I thought to myself. Yes, I liked adventure but the difference between going to a one-room schoolhouse and being bussed to the much larger, brand new school building was not a walk in the park. I called Catherine, "What time does your bus arrive at the school tomorrow? I'd like to meet up with you when we get there." She said, "Oh, that would be great, I arrive on the early bus." I said, "Oh no, my schedule says I'm on the late bus, but maybe we can eat lunch together." We checked the time for lunch and to our surprise it was the same time. I felt so relieved because I wanted to be with someone I knew. Catherine and I had been in the same schools since fourth grade and I wanted to be with a friend. This was new territory for me, and challenging for many different reasons.

Going from elementary school to junior high school was like entering a new country with completely different customs and procedures. Stepping into seventh grade that first day was overwhelming to me. The noise of students coming and going, trying to find their places sounded like Grand Central Station. I wasn't feeling very comfortable, but then this was only the first day! HA. The students in my seventh-grade class came from several different local towns. We were the first seventh grade class to be bussed to the brand-new school, called Northeastern.

It felt mammoth compared to the tiny school buildings I had experienced! At lunchtime Catherine and I talked nonstop and shared our feelings. I said, "At least they gave us a map of the school which was helpful." She said, "Yes, I'm sure it will not take us long to get used to things." I thought to myself, *I'm glad the school is divided into three wings. That makes it feel a little smaller.* Any time Catherine and I had a chance, we would compare our classes and share what we liked and disliked.

In junior high Catherine and I were in the same typing class. We laughed when we talked about the fun memories of learning to print and write in cursive in grade school and now we were learning something entirely new. I said, "This time we won't be waving our hands in the air with the up down motions. We'll be pounding keys on a machine!" We were definitely stepping into a new era. Learning to type on the keys of a typewriter was exciting; it was my first experience with this new technology! Our teacher, Mr. Pike, was a tall man who always walked around and looked over our shoulders to see if we were following directions. A little nerve-racking for me but he made it fun, so much so, that I eagerly looked forward to the first fifteen minutes of each class when we got to practice typing.

At the very beginning of the course Mr. Pike said, "First, we will learn the arrangement of the letters and where to place our fingers. Remember *F* and *J* are the two central letters where we will always place our index fingers to begin. Those two keys have a small bump on each to let you know your fingers are positioned properly. And then we'll learn the home row and where to place the rest of our fingers." After learning the placement of all the letters and numbers we began typing all kinds of scripts. Mr. Pike said, "Rule number one: never, ever look at the keyboard while typing!" I was now sweating bricks because of all the tight rules around typing, but then I should be used to rules! I had to pretend to be blindfolded as I typed! I surprised myself and found it wasn't long until I felt "at one with the typewriter." This course was a discipline and it reminded me a little of learning the straight and narrow ways and staying inside the lines at home and church. The familiarity of discipline felt good. Yes, I was in yet another new world and began to enjoy the adventure. I loved learning!

Junior high wasn't always easy but I tried to be strong and kept good friends. I knew there were many cliques among the girls but I felt blessed that there were some who befriended me and included me in their friendship circles. Living in two worlds is never easy, and I was grateful for the comfort and support of good friends at this new, public school, which was so different from life at home and church.

Our school offered industrial arts, home economics, art, music, and physical education along with the other courses. Now, many schools are dropping those subjects. So many things have changed over the years. "Life skills" were emphasized but preparing for college and the academics took priority.

Taking home economics was fun because the kitchen we used was filled with new appliances, very different from what we had at home. Mrs. Dee was very enthused about teaching and made the lessons enjoyable, but sometimes I thought it was rather humorous because my mother had already taught me how to set a table and she often brought flowers in from her garden to place for a centerpiece. That was very important to Mrs. Dee and she would say, "Always have a centerpiece and remember on which side the fork, knife, and spoon are placed." I thought to myself, *Spoon? I know where the spoon goes.* I also noticed, not one spoon in Mrs. Dee's kitchen had a sharp edge! Everything looked new. We were graded on all of our assignments. Sometimes we worked in teams and other times individually.

One day Mrs. Dee announced that there would be a cherry pie baking contest. I thought, *That sounds like a fun activity.* We practiced making pie dough and pies in class. But to make a pie on my own would be a challenge because my dough never turned out like I wanted. That week I called Catherine. I asked, "Any chance you could come to my house on Saturday to practice making the dough and cherry pie?" She said, "That sounds like fun, I'll be there around 10:00 a.m." I was so excited, because like everything else I did, I wanted to do a great job and of course wanted to win the pie baking contest!

The two of us worked in my mother's kitchen making dough, scattering flour all over the table and floor. We started laughing so hard it was difficult to complete the practice. I started singing, "Can she bake a cherry pie, Billy Boy, Billy Boy? Can she bake a cherry pie, Charming Billy? She can make a cherry pie, quick as a cat can wink her eye…" and we started laughing all over again. Believe it or not, we finally managed to make two cherry pies which were edible, but I'm not sure they would have won any contest on that day. The challenge was to learn how to make the pies by ourselves during the contest.

The day came and we all lined up at our tables getting ready. I was glad Catherine was at the other end of the room because we would have lost it thinking about our practice on Saturday. When the teacher said, "Okay, you may begin," I was ready but felt very nervous. I worked hard and managed to make the cherry pie. I actually wanted to sing again but I was in class so had to contain myself. I couldn't wait until our next class to hear who won. To my disappointment I didn't win, but I learned that practice makes better, because today, I can make a cherry pie fit for royalty.

During my junior school and high school years, there were lots of things happening in the world but for me, it usually felt like they were mostly in the background because at home we didn't discuss politics or world events. At school, we no longer had to get under our desks when practicing air-raid drills like we did in grade school, though there were certainly some other things happening that did not stay in the background.

The Vietnam war was going on and it was clear there was much emotion and conflict around it. John F. Kennedy became president and only two years later he was assassinated. I was sitting in our problems of democracy class when suddenly our teacher was notified to turn on the TV, made available for special kinds of learning, and when she did, we were all riveted to the screen in horror. "BREAKING NEWS: President John F. Kennedy has been assassinated!" Maria, who was sitting beside me, burst out crying. Even the reporter on the TV was crying. It scared me! We were all shocked and saddened. When I got home my parents said they had heard it on the radio. Not much else was said and we were all going around with our own thoughts roiling in our minds. The air was thick with grief! Lyndon Johnson became President and we listened to his speech on the radio, because my parents knew it was more than just news; it was an important historical time. The march on Washington was huge when Martin Luther King, Jr. shared his inspirational "I Have a Dream" speech just a few months before the assassination happened. Our country was in an upheaval of changes during these times, and the events made a huge impression on my mind during these school years.

By the time senior high flew around I had to sign up for driver's education. I never felt I needed it because I had learned to drive the tractor on the farm in my early teens. I remember going from one field to another and sometimes drove on the main road. I pretended I was one with the others, driving on the road and feeling very important. Sometimes I drove the car around the driveway and the barns before I was sixteen, just for practice. So driver's education didn't feel necessary and the course was a breeze. My biggest problem since then was having a heavy foot. Not good!

Many changes took place between the time I started junior high and graduated. Modern technology played a big role. Inventions seemed to move faster than lightening, from cordless telephones to minicomputers, compact discs to space exploration, and more. Living in a conservative world I often felt behind the times but I tried to keep learning and stay as informed as possible. I certainly was ready to move on as I was soon to step into another era and learn even more!

# High School Graduation

*"Education is not just about going to school and getting a degree. It's about widening your knowledge and absorbing the truth about life."* -Shakuntala Devi

It was 1964 and we were on the cusp of freedom. Graduation was right around the corner. Our class motto was "Education is the key to success that opens the door to knowledge."

Each week the anticipation grew. On Monday the principal made the announcements—"Hello seniors, this an exciting time in your lives. We will have the award assembly this Friday and remember to invite your family. The baccalaureate service will be on Sunday night at 8:00 o'clock and graduation is on Tuesday evening at 8:00 o'clock. This is your last week here at Northeastern High School, and I wish you the very best as you reach this important milestone in your life."

Friday came, and we gathered in the auditorium in the afternoon for the achievement awards. I never considered myself a scholar in school but being a hard worker helped. I had to be industrious as an ant, but I thrived on learning. I loved biology, geography, social studies, music, and home economics. To my surprise, I heard my name, "Sandra Hauck, please come forward." I thought to myself, *Is this for real?* "We are pleased to give you the award from the home economics department." Imprinted on the award, it said, "To the outstanding student in Home Economics."

Why was I surprised? Growing up on a farm, it was typical for me to be baking, cooking, and sewing! Actually, my mother should have received the award! I was touched and elated. Seeing the woman depicted on the trophy made me smile because she looked like I was feeling...proud, but modest. To this day, I will remember Mrs. Dee, the home economics teacher, as caring and one who strongly supported me on my journey. I wonder if she knew on some level how difficult it was for me to be so different from my peers? I felt her unspoken empathy. And like sunshine coming through the window, there was my mother in the audience smiling with delight.

As the big day grew nearer I was getting anxious for the event, but before graduation, we were asked to attend the baccalaureate service. The service felt like a church gathering as we sang a few hymns like "Our God, Our Help in Ages Past." A local pastor read the scripture and said a prayer. The eleventh and twelfth grade mixed chorus, looking like a flock of birds, sang "America The Beautiful." The service felt joyful but sad at the same time. Friendly faces came to help celebrate.

Finally, the evening came for graduation. I was doing cartwheels in my mind and was a bundle of nerves. I knew graduation would be a turning point for me, having more freedom and being able to make some of my own choices. At least that was my dream!

As the time approached, I thought hard about what I wanted to wear. Graduation was a huge milestone, and even though I was not allowed to attend a party afterward, I wanted to look my best. I finally decided to wear the mint green dress that I had made in home economics class. After all, I got an *A* making it, and I loved how it fit. Weighing less than 100 lbs. helped me slip right into it. A nice memory! I wore a simple pair of black shoes, low heels, with hose of course! I put my hair up as usual with every hair in place along with the very heavy prayer covering. Mother was there to help me if needed but I spent most of the time in my room by myself. My little sister peeked in now and then to see if I was making progress.

My mother, my little sister, Dawn, Grandmother Minnie, and Aunt Blanche came to my graduation. I was so happy with joy because I adored them more than they realized. They were earth angels encouraging me on my life's journey and were the strong women closest to me. For them to be present to help celebrate this special day was a gift to me that I will never forget. My father did not attend, a common theme throughout my life, but I didn't let his disapproval dampen my enthusiasm. Why he did not attend? I will never know for sure, but it was clear that our chosen pathways in life were diverging more and more as I grew older. By this time, I knew that he had strong personal and religious reasons for withholding his support, so I stepped firmly onto my own pathway with the foundational love and support of the rest of the family.

As our graduation class of 162 students whirled around in the lobby putting on their caps and gowns, there was joy in the air. This experience was good for me. I felt connected to the whole group in a way I had never felt before. We were all dressed the same, and there was a feeling of belonging. I realized this was a group of people I would always remember and hold dear.

The procession began with the "Pomp and Circumstance March" as our class paraded down the aisle, feeling ever so important. We sat in the front rows, and for a short time, I saw this body of students in a different light. They were smart, kindhearted, and most had bright futures ahead of them. We felt a glow of light among us. Everything became quiet as the speakers lined up and the chorus bellowed out, "If Thou but Suffer God to Guide Thee" and "Brother James's Air." Is that why I still love the 23rd Psalm today?

Dr. Don McGarey gave the commencement address, our principal, Mr. Sutton, presented our class, and finally, our supervising principal, Mr. Orendorf, gave out the diplomas. One by one we marched to the podium and received our recognition. After earning my diploma, I was on cloud nine and could not wait to aim for higher things. Graduation was a huge milestone for me! I was more than excited to move on and find my own way. It is what most of us understand as FREEDOM.

Our class song was called "Climb Every Mountain." And I agree with Dr. Seuss who said, "You're off to Great Places, Today is your day! Your mountain is waiting, So...get on your way." How true that was for me even though there were so many unknowns! The audience stood as our class proceeded to march out into the big lobby but bigger yet, was the march out into the real world, on to the many unknowns for each of us.

Of course I was not allowed to attend the prom or other parties. Even if I'd been allowed to go, it was apparent to me that I would not fit in, and furthermore, I've never heard anyone say they loved being a wallflower. Don't get me wrong—secretly I wanted to dance the night away and join the fun, but I kept my focus on the flip side, which was that I had secured an excellent education and made wonderful friends along the way. I continue to keep in touch with some of those classmates to this day.

Education is a real gift, and I am thankful for all my learning experiences! Graduation does not mean that we stop learning. After that special milestone, I became acutely aware of how life's lessons continued, and it was up to me to find my path, follow my dreams, and make good choices. My education helped me become empowered and enabled me to become a critical thinker and ask questions. Yes, there were bumps in the road and all kinds of challenges, but I never gave up. Graduation was a milestone and will always be symbolic of freedom for me, not necessarily freedom from school or from institutional education, but the freedom to choose for myself as an adult—the freedom to spread my own wings with additional learning and experience as their foundation.

# The Butterfly Kiss

*Kisses are the flowers of love in bloom...*
~Author Unknown

Some called it "puppy love." Others said, "They are just children and it won't last." Funny, how some people presume to know volumes as they express their personal opinions.

Carlton and I were preschoolers when we first laid eyes on each other. Our mothers claimed they held us on their laps in the same pew when we went to church. Year after year, we would cross paths and then I turned fourteen and he was thirteen.

Every chance we had, we made sure we talked—about school, friends, and how life wasn't always fair. Our parents allowed us to spend time together as long as we were with our youth group or family. In other words, no dating until I was sixteen.

In the winter when we wanted to go sledding, ice skating, or have fun in the snow, we rounded up our friends and met at our neighbor's farm, where there was a lovely pond. This was one of the best ways just to be together in our town of Starview. At the pond, Carlton would take time to help me put on my skates and often gave me one of his hand warmers to put inside my glove. My favorite game while skating was "Crack the Whip," where a long line of skaters hold hands and the leader takes them snaking back and forth all over the ice, until suddenly the leader turns, and the line whips around, snapping the last few skaters so fast that it's hard to hold on. I would always ask to be on the end of the line. Carlton would be beside me in case I let go and landed in a snowdrift, and sometimes I landed there on purpose so that he could help me get up. He always radiated kindness and even at thirteen, he showed a gentlemen's maturity.

Going to Bible school every evening for the last two weeks of summer was fun because it was another way we could spend time together. After class, he would go across the road to the little country store and return with a Hershey candy bar to slip in my hand before I left for home. I still have the wrappers, always a reminder of his thoughtfulness.

After a year of our "puppy love" I called him one night and suggested that we break up, and he simply replied, "Okay." I thought maybe we should give ourselves space because we were so young. For three years we went our separate ways, but always kept an eye on each other. Later I learned Carlton was disappointed that we broke up but was happy when we got back together, and I was too.

After my senior year in high school, we reconnected and started dating. Our first date was quite memorable. We took a ride in his convertible sports car down along the Susquehanna River. We had a serious talk about getting back together again. In my mind and dreams I always wished for a smart, good looking, and caring guy, one who was taller than I, and one who "walked the talk." We agreed we were ready to begin a new adventure together.

After the ride, we returned to my house and had ice cream and cake, a tradition when dating. As we stood in the doorway when he was ready to go home, he gently put his arms around me. He placed a "butterfly kiss" ever so gently on my cheek and it has lasted forever.

We announced our engagement on February 14th 1966, and we got married on June10th 1967. June 10th, 2018, we celebrated our 51st anniversary. After all these years, I realize I was blessed with the gift of Carlton's presence in my life. We have been on an interesting journey together. His partnership is invaluable, and his kisses are still appreciated with love and tenderness.

# Staying Inside the Lines

*"They love to tell you Stay inside the lines But something's better On the other side." -*John Mayer

I have found that the path of religion has not always been smooth.

When I was very young, I was like a sponge, taking in my surroundings and noticing beauty everywhere. Whenever I was lucky enough to spend time with a jumbo box of Crayola crayons and its rainbow of colors, I was in heaven. Colors were fascinating to me. There were other art supplies, such as dull colored pencils, markers, pens, and cheap paint to use, but crayons were my favorite. I was captivated by the bright colors and enjoyed the texture of the crayons.

I soon discovered while coloring, that if I blended red and yellow, magically they turned into orange, the glow of sunshine and warmth. If I mixed blue, green, and red, I created darker colors, for showing night and darkness.

When I was growing up on the farm, there was always plenty of work to be done. But on rainy days, Mother would suggest that we get out the crayons and coloring books. Most of the books were filled with pictures of animals, buildings, vehicles, and plenty of Bible story characters. What keeps ringing in my ears is my mother saying, "Stay inside the lines, Sandra." I heard the same thing at school when my teacher would say, "Stay inside the lines when you color." This statement was so ingrained in my mind that it became a metaphor for my life's journey.

There was a time during my elementary school years when Mother gave me a box of paper dolls. I spent time admiring the fancy dresses, skimpy underwear, darling shoes, and frilly socks. These were things I wasn't allowed to have. I began wondering why I was allowed to play with these art line images but could not have beautiful clothing like that in real life. "Bright and gaudy things are worldly," my parents said, but having crayons, and coloring with bright colors was acceptable, thank goodness. As I grew older, I became acutely aware that home and the church were filled with strict rules. Many of these teachings made me start to question silently in my mind, but I knew not to ask out loud. More confusion continued in my life.

Handcrafts, like embroidery, sewing, and cooking were encouraged and acceptable. Beautiful embroidery work was lovingly incorporated into pillowcases and tablecloths, but artwork just for the sake of beauty and creativity was not encouraged and definitely not to be placed on the walls. Sewing and cooking were necessary and functional skills, so those talents were encouraged. The leaders of the church justified the rules though they didn't make sense to me. I wondered, weren't the crafts we made, art?

Art, for example, was not discussed or encouraged in our home. After I attended middle and high school, I became more attuned to what real art was about. At that time, though, I wasn't very interested. I was firmly in the habit of "staying inside the lines," only doing what I was told to do. This kind of teaching did not allow for much freedom of thought or self-expression.

I often struggled with life's contradictions and hypocrisy. To me, there was the promise of so much freedom in color, but I found that when I tried to mix my beautiful colors with the dogma of religion, the colors just became shadowed and muddy. There was beauty all around me, including the bright, brilliant colors of nature, but it felt like the doctrine restricted my appreciation of beauty whether natural or man-made.

Research has demonstrated that coloring can be a therapeutic exercise for young and older people. But my experience of staying inside the lines made me live in fear of immodesty, and afraid of making mistakes.

"Stay inside the lines, Sandra," is a message from my early years. After graduation, especially, I bravely started replacing it with "What if I explore beyond the lines?" and found out for myself what works best for me. Exploring creativity took courage. I am glad I learned to appreciate functionality alongside color and beauty, and was taught right from wrong, but I'm also glad I learned that life is more than staying inside the lines.

Ironically, I majored in art education, eventually graduating with a Master's degree. I discovered while teaching art, an enjoyment of what I had missed in my younger years. I loved encouraging students to create and express their God-given ideas. Life has a way of teaching us as we progress through it, and I'm glad I had the opportunity to pursue my dreams and encourage others to pursue theirs.

# Are My Seams Straight?

*"Today, you can decide to walk in freedom. You can choose to walk differently. You can walk as a free person, enjoying every step."* ~Thich Nhat Hanh

In the 1920s, as hemlines of dresses and skirts rose, and churches were not heated, women began to wear flesh-colored stockings for warmth. They were first made of silk or rayon, and after 1940 they were made of nylon.

I was born in 1946, and by the time I was a teenager I was introduced to nylons, and some, with seams. If you've never heard of this style, the nylons had seams all the way down the back, from the top of the stocking to the heel. At first, I wasn't a real fan but soon became accustomed to wearing them. The funny thing was, I thought those seams enhanced my legs and looked rather sexy. How did that fit into the realm of not looking worldly? I wore dresses that came to just below my knees and nylons with low-heeled shoes. In my home, the emphasis was to cover your skin, especially arms and legs. Although, I remember Mother making our bathing suits, and thank goodness, they did not have to cover our arms and legs. Things kept creeping into my life that did not make sense! My job was to figure out what worked for me.

One day when I was getting ready to go out for a particular event, I remember asking my sister, "Hey sis, will you please check if my seams are straight?" "Yes," she said, "they look lovely." For me, that was very important because I wanted to look just right, even though by nature I didn't feel particularly prim or proper, nor sophisticated. It was that perfectionist side of me that wanted everything to look just right.

The emphasis on dressing a certain way was a big part of my life, up until I was twenty-one. No slacks, no shorts, dresses below the knee—no way would I dream of showing off my knees, but then I didn't think they were attractive anyway, kind of knobby looking to me. So why all the fuss about how we were expected to dress and why was wearing nylons with seams acceptable? Was it because the men of our religion wanted to protect us by keeping us covered up?

Which particular family and religious group we grew up in made all the difference in what we were allowed or not allowed to do. Later in life, I discovered I wasn't the only one in a religious group who was required to dress differently. Not only Mennonites, but also Buddhist monks, nuns, Catholic priests, Orthodox Jews, Sikh's, Mormon missionaries, the Amish, and many more, had well-established dress codes. What I learned about myself was that the restrictions of our church felt detrimental to me, since I didn't have a choice about participating; I felt forced, out of fear that was instilled in me from an early age. Because I didn't genuinely believe it was right for me, I felt this part of my world was sideways of the concept of reality in my heart. For a long time, it kept me from feeling I had the right to be authentic.

This topic of dress and religion is interesting to me. I find it ironic that there was so much emphasis on hiding behind clothing, according to man's rules, when, at the same time, we were taught that we were created perfect and whole. Oh, I believe in modesty, but there was never an emphasis on appreciating ourselves. Was how we looked more important than focusing on the joy of living? With the emphasis on our looks and blending in, I felt keenly the absence of any discussion on how to accept and focus on our inherent, God-given qualities of goodness and beauty.

I laugh when I think about the many times these self-admonitions have followed me: "I have to do it properly," "I may not mess up," and "I must stay inside the lines." Because I was taught through fear and intimidation, these are the recriminations that have been hard to delete from my mind. I became very self-conscious about almost everything! It took me years to transform those old habits of thinking. I don't always wear stockings with my dresses these days, but I can be hard on myself if I mess up and make a mistake. I quickly practice turning that around and tell myself, "It's okay, life happens," and have learned to move on without the guilt.

To me, the whole idea is that we are born into this world for a reason, and it's up to each of us to figure out why. I no longer have to ask "Are my seams straight?" but I often ask myself if I'm at peace with life and doing my part to make a difference in this world. I choose to focus on what I've learned to hold as important.

# Fault Lines and Tremors

*"I feel like we need to be aware of the ways we use and misuse religious dogma: whether it takes us deeper into love and inclusion or it separates us." ~*Sue Monk Kidd

As I was growing up, I began to realize that our home life wasn't typical, but then what is typical? Conservative Mennonite tradition has a life of its own, depending on how the devotees interpret the guidelines.

In my home, religion played a huge role in our family's life. My parents' religion felt very restrictive to me as I got into my late teens. Rules, rules, rules! There were rifts, cracks, and fractures as I tried to formally follow my parents' guidelines. The tremors came when I began questioning "the truths" regarding what was right and wrong. How could there be such a long list of wrongdoings? "Don't swear," they said, so I did, while working in the garden. I had to hear how it sounded. "Don't wear jewelry because it only brings attention to yourself." So I did. I made rings, bracelets, and necklaces out of dandelions, secretly. "Don't wear lipstick." So I did. When Easter came, I used red jellybeans and painted my lips ruby red, the brightest ever, in the secret haven of my bedroom. The list goes on. I was growing and I needed to test these guidelines.

My mother was loving, kind-hearted, and a devout Christian. She lived by example as she helped my father raise their seven children. She loved to sing, recite scripture, and knew how to laugh. She had solid work ethics and taught us what work meant for our futures. Mother, like all mothers, had flaws, but she was able to conquer her challenges in a quiet way. In my memories, I can still see her occasionally exiting the kitchen in tears, going into another room to be alone, and probably to pray when she was feeling down.

My father was challenging to relate to. For my dad, church and family were a complicated mix, from what I observed. For him to become part of the leadership of the church, he felt it was important to make sure his family followed every rule. Inevitably, at times, we fell short though we tried our best, and at these times, we felt his frustration with us. Sometimes it felt like we children were trapped inside a birdcage, trying to figure out what these teachings meant, and we struggled to find freedom. Each of us handled the challenges differently. The joy was that we could at least see out of the birdcage to learn. As my older siblings each left home and got married, they gave themselves permission to seek out different churches to join and interpretations of the doctrine that they felt comfortable with. All seven of us children left the Mennonite church. Funny, when love and care are the core of a religion, it can set a person free.

Reflecting on those memories, it felt like I was walking on shaky ground. I observed in my parents, a loving mother, in contrast to a father who was intensely demanding. Unfortunately, it became apparent to me as I grew older that my father's ambitions may have played rather a large part in what he was trying to teach us. Steeping himself in his own interpretation of this conservative religion, with the ambition of leadership within the church complicated matters. The confluence often became a whirlpool. I believe there is a place for all people, and I have great respect for all religions if their core is love, forgiveness, and living peacefully. I was taught to hold Christ as my example, but in my reality, I found that the man-made rules and dogma seemed to fog over that beautiful light and glow of the Divine.

Later in life, as an adult, I took the time to search for more answers so that I could see clearly and live a life of joy. In fact, one of my favorite songs is "I Can See Clearly Now." I sometimes felt like a volcano spewing out questions and feelings about the contradictions and the long list of things that I could not make sense of. It was therapeutic to discuss controversial issues with others whom I trusted, and discover answers that felt right to me. Fear and guilt were a waste of energy to me, because they kept me stuck like a caged little bird.

For me, it has been essential to find out what is behind the cloth, the teachings, and the Holy Scriptures of religion. I had to figure out if the rules and regulations were man-made or if they truly originated from the Divine. The contradictions I experienced felt misleading, as well as damaging to my spiritual journey. I believe in a higher power, and that the Divine is with us if we choose. Christ often asked questions rather than giving answers. To me, that is profound. It shows me that we were given a mind to think for ourselves. The Holy Spirit or the Divine Spirit cannot work within us if we allow ourselves to be shut down by man-made rules and dogma.

I am thankful for all of the good that I experienced in my growing up years, and there was plenty. And, after sorting through the heap of teachings and doing my personal work, I found a wave of peace, in contrast to the fear I had experienced for so many years. To "walk the talk," with an open and loving heart takes practice, wisdom, and discernment. When it comes to religion, I feel it is very important to be true to myself and to listen directly to the Divine. I count my many blessings and am most grateful for those who have offered love and support on my journey.

## PART THREE

# Taking Big Risks

*"Go out on a limb. That's where the fruit is."* ~Jimmy Carter

# Marriage

*"It's not about the cards you're dealt, - but how you play the hand."*
~Randy Pausch

We met when we were children. Yes, he was the one who sat on his mother's lap in church beside me sitting in my own mother's lap when we were just toddlers. His mother often said to me, "I always wished for a little girl with curls like you." She had two sons. That was the beginning, and Carlton and I laugh today, thinking maybe there was an arranged marriage happening, and we didn't know it.

We dated seriously after high school. We were young and in love. He was going to college, and I was working. After he finished his first two years of college, we announced our engagement.

We were encouraged to read books about marriage, and some of our married friends gave their opinions of what marriage was like from their own experiences. We were entering unknown territory, as all marriages encompass, regardless of prior experience. We were sure we wanted to get married, and it was exciting. This was taking a risk, but we certainly didn't think so at the time.

On our wedding day, June 10, 1967, we were all getting ready for the happy occasion. Once again my mother came through with her love and support, but my father decided not to participate, nor walk me down the aisle, because he had a list of things he didn't approve of. I was hurt, but he had his own agenda, and I was strong enough to stick to mine. I managed to continue with our plans. I walked down the aisle alone, into the arms of my wonderful young man. That was all that mattered on that special day, and it was one of the happiest days in my life.

We decided to move to State College, Pennsylvania, after our honeymoon in the Great Smoky Mountains of Tennessee. He would finish his education at Penn State University, and I would work. We thoroughly loved living in this small town and we loved the university. The big red brick house that we lived in was lovely. We rented the first floor, and a few students rented the second and third floors.

We had wonderful neighbors. On one side lived an elderly lady who was friendly and was impressed with the small garden that I put in. She loved gardening as well, with rows of vegetables and an array of colorful flowers near her house. She enjoyed canning and worked hard to keep everything in order. Right before we moved, she gave me her canner after learning that I knew how to use one.

She too hung her wash outside on the washing line, so I felt comfortable doing the same thing. Until one morning I wasn't too sure I should. I went out to get the clothing down from the wash line and noticed all my underwear was missing. I laughed to myself and figured a student had played a prank. I knew it wasn't dear Mrs. Neeley! Later I read in a police report that someone, probably a student, was stealing clothing from wash lines and I realized I was an easy target being so close to the main street.

The neighbors who lived on the other side of our house were also lovely people. Mr. Norris was an English professor at Penn State University. His wife was a talented harpist, and I loved hearing her play her harp. Sometimes I would visit to watch her play and be mesmerized, listening to the beautiful melodies. She looked absolutely angelic as she played.

Living in town was fun but different. We had the cutest garage behind our house, and it was great to be able to park our 1963 VW Bug there, especially in bad weather. However, one morning I went to the garage and noticed that our car was missing! Panic set in as I thought, *Not too long ago I had some wash stolen!* I knew we had parked the car in the garage the night before.

I went back into the house and woke Carlton, saying, "You won't believe this, but our car is not in the garage!" He said, "No way, it has to be there." He got up, and we both went out to look, and as I had told him, it wasn't there. We decided to go in front of the house to look along the street. To our shock, we saw that someone had taken our little car and put it right on our front porch! We laughed and then realized we were not sure how to get it off of the porch. Later, several of the students who rented upstairs came down and confessed, and helped move it back to where it belonged. This was life in a university town, where pranks could be fun but also risky! They were lucky that we hadn't yet called the police and we both had a good sense of humor.

We found a church we liked nearby and made more connections with wonderful people. We didn't have to go far for music concerts, the arts, sports, and shows. Our first two years of marriage were so much fun, and sometimes it felt like "playing house." I enjoyed my work, and Carlton enjoyed his studies. Our goal was for him to finish his education before we started having children. He paid his way through college, so I was willing to work and not add any extra expenses while he finished. Although I longed to go to college, I kept that dream for later.

At this point in our marriage, life was good, and we were enjoying the adventure. I tried to be supportive of his goals and dreams. He graduated with high honors, and we were both proud and thankful. Now he was anticipating working in the real world. Carlton's first job was working at Arthur Andersen & Co. in Washington D.C. Our second move was to Fairfax, Virginia where we lived for a year. I was now pregnant with our first child.

Fifty years later I have no regrets about marrying this wonderful man. Who would? He has been my rock and encouraged me never to give up. Needless to say, like all marriages, we had our challenges during those early years. In our twenties and thirties, we were still trying to find ourselves and figure out things that we'd never faced before. We discovered, of course, that having children also added more challenges. That was just part of the risk that came with every new experience.

For us, marriage was not simply giving 50-50, it has been 100-100 and giving everything we had of ourselves to the commitment. Over the years, I have come to realize that marriage is a spiritual adventure in which each partner sacrifices for the other for the good of the relationship. The relationship represents the oneness that the two become. It is about sharing joys and sorrows, working as a team. I believe there's no such thing as a perfect couple or a perfect marriage. It took both of us to work and learn how to improve our relationship. Professional help along the way added tools for better communication. We learned to see life differently as the years went by. Like life, marriage is one big adventure, and it takes two to work, learn, and stay committed.

# The Angel with a Halo

*"One's true worth as a human being is not a matter of*
*outward appearance or title but derives rather from the*
*breadth of one's spirit. Everything comes down to faith and*
*conviction. It is what is in one's heart and the substance of*
*one's actions that count."* ~Daisaku Ikeda

Even after my husband and I got married, I was still wearing the "prayer covering." I was now in new territory: marriage and living in a different town. For the first time I lived away from home and the church I belonged to. My prayer covering felt heavier and heavier, making me feel more self-conscious and embarrassed. Who really cared? I did. I tried my best to follow the rules of the church but to keep the prayer covering on, just wasn't me. I found that doing something I didn't believe in was a very rocky road to travel.

At this point in life I began thinking more for myself, giving myself permission to consider my feelings and ask more questions. Like cherry blossoms in springtime, I felt positive, new growth appearing. Spring changes into summer and my life was following that same path. Figuring out how to make changes, after making many promises to the church, was huge for me. After two decades of dogma I had to discover for myself what was best for me so I could live in peace. In no way did I want to shed my faith, because I always believed in a higher power, but my challenge over the years was to define what that meant, for myself, and how to blend it comfortably into my life and self-expression.

While my husband went to school, completing his undergraduate work, I got a job with a justice of the peace. I worked beside another girl who was a lot of fun and we worked well together. Our responsibilities were many, but mainly involved processing tickets that were hand delivered by the police officers. In and out the officers came, usually friendly and on a mission to get their work done.

One day while I was working in the office, in walked a police officer. He said, "Good morning, Mr. Donnely, oh, and over there she sits, the angel with a halo." I was so embarrassed and could only give him a faint smile as I said, "Good morning." That was the heaviest my prayer covering ever felt, except for maybe the time I had sat next to that senior boy in high school. I was not an angel, and at that moment the police officer's comment struck a chord that triggered the pain of struggling with being different all over again. I didn't want to go through the rest of my life trying to be someone I wasn't.

I went home that day with a heavy heart and an even heavier prayer covering. In fact, as soon as my husband got home I cried and I said, "Dearie, do I have to wear this prayer covering when I don't think it's necessary? I can pray anywhere, with or without this covering." He looked at me with his smiling eyes, and said, "Of course not, if you don't want to." I was so relieved and couldn't believe how easy it was. I thought all along I had to wear it forever because of the promise I had made in church. Growing up in an environment where men made the rules, I was used to asking permission on numerous things, and I felt so relieved that my husband was much more supportive of my happiness as an individual than how "following the rules" looked to others. As I took off the prayer covering, I actually felt like a new person, more like the part of me I had been hiding: my true self.

It wasn't until after I got married that I took off the prayer covering for good. Now the weight of the millstone around my neck was much lighter. I only felt a tad of guilt. According to how my father interpreted the rules of the church I belonged to, I broke a promise, and of course that was judged and looked down upon. My parents reluctantly accepted my decision, but I knew they were not pleased. I always felt the prayer covering was something that had no purpose for me. On the other hand, my mother often said she felt protected by wearing it. I respected her view but never felt

158

the same way. I believe in a higher power that works in mysterious ways. We each can choose what we want to believe and do. For me, I was now on a different path with the Divine guiding me. I discovered that to find authenticity, one has to be honest and vulnerable.

# What? You Cut Your Hair?

*"Why don't you get a haircut? You look like a chrysanthemum."* ~P. G. Wodehouse

I hung onto my long hair for 20 years or may I say it hung on me. I never had a strong desire to keep it long, but because of the way I was raised, I was torn between wanting to cut it and conforming to the rules of keeping it long. As I grew into adulthood, the urge to cut my hair increased until it was practically irresistible. Then after Carlton and I were married, I seriously wanted to cut my hair, but I was still learning the ropes within this union. What was I was allowed to do? I was so ready to make changes on my own and to ask for permission felt frustrating. It was not in my nature to want someone to tell me what to do. I wanted to be equal. So, to ask my husband if I could cut my hair felt uncomfortable, and I kept my desire to myself, at least for a little while.

During the first three years of our marriage, my hair was still long, almost to my waist. I remember the first time I went to the hair salon and the girl who was going to wash my hair, asked, "Don't you want it cut?" I said, "No, please just style it." I wanted to say, "Yes I want it cut!" but I didn't have the nerve. It was hilarious because the girl decided to style my long hair into a beehive and believe me the bees would have loved it. In the 1960s teasing the hair to create volume was typical. So when Carlton dropped me off at the hair salon, I entered as Sandra Miller, dutiful, plain, obedient wife and daughter, but I came out Audrey Hepburn in *Breakfast at Tiffany's!*

When Carlton came to pick me up after work, he did not recognize me as I was standing on the sidewalk waiting. He drove right by me. He soon realized it was me and he turned around to stop and pick me up. We were both laughing hysterically but I was thinking, *I should have let the girl cut my hair!* When I got home, it didn't take me long to decide to undo all her hard work. However, it took me a very long time to free the crazy style, because of all the hair teasing she had done. What I thought would be my perk for that day turned out to be a waste of time and money. Go figure, a hive with my long hair!

Just in case you are wondering what a beehive hairdo looks like, imagine the shape of a gray wasps' nest. The width at the top of the nest is broad and narrows down where the bees enter at the bottom. For my hairstyle that day, the girl took a layer of hair closest to my scalp and turned it into a huge bun to create height. She then took the top layer of my hair and teased and combed it over the bun making it even higher. Teased hair was popular during the 1960s and you can go online to see how it is done. It certainly creates volume, but what it does to the hair itself is quite the operation to undo.

I gradually began wearing shorter hairstyles after that experience. But it wasn't noticeable until after I discarded the prayer covering. I knew my parents would not approve, but Carlton was okay with my choice. I was in new territory now and little by little I was finding my own way. Carlton had never encountered these issues before. He had no sisters, just one brother. He only saw his mother's long hair, which she never cut. I'm sure she explained it to him, why she wore it long—she followed the expectations of the church, just as I was taught.

Later, when Carlton and I ventured to Bolivia, and lived there for two and half years, my hair was just below shoulder length. While I was in Bolivia, a good friend suggested I get a pixie haircut! She thought I'd look great with that style. I remember getting it cut really short and I just loved the freedom of it. When I sent pictures home to my parents, I made sure my photos were tiny to hide my hair cut. Crazy, but I only felt guilty now when I was in the presence of my parents. After all, the drill came from them and their interpretation of the scripture: "But if a woman have long hair, it is a glory to her: for her hair is given her for a covering."[1] I respected the scriptures but the interpretations were confusing to me as a woman.

When we returned home to the U.S., I made sure my hair was no shorter than shoulder length, but it wasn't long after that, I chose to do my hair the way I wanted. My dad had died while we lived in Bolivia, so I no longer had to worry about conforming to his expectations or falling short if I chose to express myself differently. Yes, it was very freeing to step into my hard-won capabilities for making my own decisions. I wanted to enjoy deciding for myself but it took some years to become comfortable with that!

This story might sound extreme and stepping into the freedoms of adulthood and sovereignty as a human being certainly felt that way to me. As much as I wanted to enjoy my spiritual journey, the dos and don'ts and trying to stay in the lines with my long hair, yet in style with the beehives, got in the way. If birds of a feather flock together, I often felt like I was in the wrong flock. As I flew from branch to branch finding my way, I learned valuable lessons. Never to give up stays at the top of the list!

Staying with my flock of earth angels and the Divine gives me hope each day. I am very thankful I married someone from the same religion even though he did not experience what I did. Being a guy, and having less strict parents made a huge difference for him. Thankfully, he has always given me support and encouraged me to make my own choices. That being said, it took years for me to undo many of those early parental and clerical scripts. Styles come and go, and you can be sure you will never see me with a beehive hairstyle again!

---

[1] 1 Corinthians 11:15

# Our Two Gems

*"What it's like to be a parent: It's one of the hardest things you'll ever do, but in exchange, it teaches you the meaning of unconditional love."* ~Nicholas Sparks

I knew I wanted children, maybe as many as four, and the two that we did have turned out to be just right. My husband and I discussed very little about parenting, but we agreed on the number of children we wanted. Funny how some things we handled a bit backwards, like not discussing the world of parenting before starting our own family, not thinking in detail about what might be involved before we threw ourselves into parenthood. I wondered, *How did my parents decide to have seven children? How does anyone know how many to have, and when is the right time?* My mother made it look so easy! As I reflect on her strength, I marvel at how well she took on the most difficult, albeit rewarding, job of a lifetime—raising children. One time I asked her, "How did you and Dad decide on having seven children?" She replied, "In those days you just accepted the children that came, and there was not a lot of discussion or control as to how many."

Shortly before Carlton's college graduation, he had to decide where he would complete the requirement of a three-month internship with an accounting firm. He could go anywhere in the U.S. He asked me, "How would you like to go to Phoenix, Arizona?" I was thrilled and said, "Yes, that would be great since my brother and family live there." So, taking off in our reliable VW, we sped away and moved to Phoenix.

We found a small apartment not far from my brother and his family. I looked forward to babysitting my niece and nephew who were little darlings. My brother and his wife helped our transition go smoothly. My brother said, "We're glad you are here, let us know how we can help you." My sister-in-law was great with making lists of places we might enjoy seeing, like museums, art galleries, and areas to hike. Almost every weekend they took us to great restaurants and sightseeing. Nadine would ask, "How would you like to go see the Desert Botanical Garden and take a few hikes this weekend?" "Yes," we said, "we want to see as much as possible." Three months flew by very quickly!

With all the hiking, we soon learned that the desert is a world of its own, with plenty of cactus, an array of colorful flowers, tons of sand, and yes, lizards and snakes. The trails twisted all through the desert, which was fun to hike, "But watch out for the snakes," my brother Dave would remind us. He knew I was jumpy when I encountered snakes, so he was looking out for me. We hiked Camelback Mountain and visited Superstition Mountain. The view from the top of South Mountain overlooking Phoenix was awesome! The perfect time to live in the Phoenix area is during the winter months when the temperatures are comfortable. We loved the climate and to see clear skies almost every day was fantastic! Arizona was a place we would return to often.

All too soon, it was time to travel back to Pennsylvania. I said to Carlton, "Our VW will be packed to the gills with all these purchases from Phoenix." I loved learning about the Native Americans and bought many books and a lot of souvenirs. *I wonder if our neighbor back home would appreciate this bowl made by a Native American,* I thought to myself as I pursued the open markets. What fun to share these treasures from such a beautiful place!

During the last month we lived in Arizona I was not feeling well. Could this be how it felt to be pregnant? On our trip home, I now laugh, because I wasn't sure, so I drank a lot of ginger ale and even sipped a little Pepto-Bismol. As soon as we arrived home in State College, I made an appointment with my doctor for the next day. After I gave the information he needed, the doctor said, "You're having morning sickness!" The doctor would not give me any medicine before my first three months were up so I continued to feel miserable. Day after day I was sick, and by the third month, I had to quit my job because of morning sickness. I was not a happy trooper because the sickness continued throughout the whole nine months. I managed somehow, and no matter how bad I felt each month, I was, nonetheless, so excited about having our first child.

Carlton graduated in May, 1969. His graduation from Penn State University was a real highlight for both of us. I asked him, "Are you excited about your big day?" He said, "I am very glad to be finished and to move on." We welcomed his parents and his only brother and his wife for the graduation events. His brother and wife had met at Penn State while they were students so this event was extra exciting for everyone. We were so proud as we watched Carlton, as marshal, leading the graduating class of the College of Business across the field at Beaver Stadium. Carlton was a hard-working student and it paid off; he graduated at the top of his class. His parents always stressed the importance of going to college and getting a good education. I viewed that as a gift from his parents. After the ceremonies, we went out to celebrate and ate at the much beloved, local Dutch Pantry restaurant.

With Carlton's graduation, it was time to move again! Leaving State College was bittersweet, but we took many good memories with us. We moved to Fairfax, Virginia, and rented a cozy house out in the country with nature all around us! Carlton began working for the Arthur Andersen Accounting Firm, close by, in Washington D.C. One day he came home and announced, "The company has asked me to go to Chicago for a week of training in the auditing of financial services companies" I said I understood and hoped the week would fly by quickly! His presence during my pregnancy was such a comfort and I missed him while he was gone. I decided to call my sisters and ask them to stay with me for a few days while he was away. I was so happy to have company because I still didn't know anyone in the area. They were my earth angels and they knew all about being pregnant, as they both had children of their own.

On November 11, 1969, our first daughter was born in the Fairfax Hospital. We named her Ilisa Marie. What a joy to have a beautiful daughter whom we adored. She had shiny, black hair and beautiful brown eyes. She was a darling! My mother often mentioned how blessed she was to have seven children with perfect features, including small ears. HA! Carlton and I looked at Ilisa and we also often said to each other, "How fortunate that she has perfect features...and small ears." I was a stay-at-home mom during that time and enjoyed the adventure. Ilisa slept well at night, took naps during the day, and was a very contented baby. I loved listening to her coo and making her smile. She was so much fun to watch over, and to see how quickly she learned new things was exciting. When Carlton got home from work each evening, I could not wait to tell him what she had done that day. "You wouldn't believe how strong she was as she tried pulling herself up in her crib!" He said, "Cool, good for her!" From the start, he was a big cheerleader and fan of both of our daughters.

I bought a baby book to keep a record of Ilisa's progress. On one page it explained what to expect, and on the page across from that, I kept a record of her achievements. We were so proud of how she made progress and developed into an active little girl with her very own personality. We were grateful and realized she was a gift. Soon she expressed her "Ooh's" and "Ahh's" and was crawling. We loved her more than life itself.

Whether she knew it or not, our Ilisa had been born into an adventurous family, and when she was eight months old, we moved once again, this time to Bolivia, South America, to do volunteer work. "You are going where?" our family asked and looked a little surprised, to say the least. We had always wanted to serve somewhere to help others, and we felt this was the right time to go. Although we were concerned about taking our little one, we felt confident. We were taking another risk, yes, but to us, it was an adventure not to be denied. By then, Ilisa was walking and beginning to talk. She was a real trooper, and we were so proud of her as she adapted to the new culture. This adventure was huge for each of us, and as a family, we tried to be creative and work together for the benefit of all.

Shortly after we moved to Santa Cruz, Bolivia, we settled into our home near the Mennonite Central Committee office. This was a complex surrounded by a wall. Walls were very common near the city. In our complex there were two homes and the main office with rooms for guests. Carlton was assigned the position of assistant director, and I was assigned the role of hostess while we lived there for two and half years. We felt very fortunate to live in this home that had been recently built, because it included several amenities that most of the workers who lived in the *campo* (country) didn't have. We tried to make them feel at home when they came to the city for supplies and stayed there; it was a long and arduous trip for them. I was happy I brought recipes from the States. If anyone got a little homesick for food from back home, I tried to provide some familiar things like pies, cakes, and breakfast treats. We loved the Bolivian food but appreciated a touch of home as well.

We hired Carmen, a lovely Bolivian woman. She was responsible for helping with Ilisa and doing the housework, while I was in charge of cooking and hospitality duties for our family and for the workers and guests who regularly visited from out of town. How fortunate we were to have Carmen help us. She was a hard worker and was wonderfully devoted to caring for Ilisa. I remember when she started to teach her Spanish, Ilisa would look at me and speak English and look at Carmen and speak Spanish. Ilisa also picked up Spanish as she spent time with many of her neighborhood friends. She seemed to enjoy her life and was a happy child.

Two and half years seemed to fly by and watching Ilisa grow, learn, and relate to her Bolivian friends was such fun to be a part of. She was amazing. Her childhood was very different from mine in that she had much less restriction and much greater exposure to the big, wide world.

Ilisa loved using crayons and any time she gave me a piece of paper with her drawings on it, I displayed it on the wall, tacking it to my corkboard, old-style church rules suitably overcome! One day Ilisa was in the hallway looking at her work. I thought, *What was that noise?* I ran from the kitchen upon hearing that strange sound, to see what she was doing. To my horror, she had pulled one of her papers down, and when she did, the tack fell onto the floor. She had picked it up and put it in her mouth, and yes, swallowed it! "Oh my goodness Ilisa! What are we going to do?" I exclaimed. She didn't seem like she was in pain but I made sure she sat still. At that time, my husband was on a business trip, out of town for a few days. I was alone all day. I waited until our director got home to ask for help since I wasn't used to our environment yet. It was almost midnight when he arrived, and the hours passed like centuries. After I informed him of what had happened, he suggested going to the clinic first thing in the morning. It was a sleepless night in Santa Cruz, waiting yet more centuries for the clinic to open!

The next morning I was feeling anxious as we raced to the clinic. It was "hurry up and wait" as we found ourselves standing in a long line of others seeking medical help. My nerves were ready to explode, but somehow I kept my mother's calm. Finally, we got in to see the doctor, and he took an x-ray. Low and behold, we could see the tack clear as crystal shown on the x-ray with the point of it straight up. The doctor gave Ilisa some medicine so that she could safely pass it. He said, "Please return to the clinic in five hours and we'll take another x-ray." Those five hours felt like an eternity! We returned, and they took another x-ray. There it was! That tack showed up again, but this time it looked flat, not pointy. The chemical reaction of the medicine was working to coat that sharp little tip. Fortunately, she passed the tack soon after. I rejoiced, realizing the guardian angels were watching over us. I will always be grateful for the kind people who helped in our time of need! And for Ilisa's indomitable digestive tract. Such were the unforeseen adventures of parenthood.

Thumbtacks notwithstanding, my husband and I were undaunted in our joy of parenting, and during our last months of living in Bolivia, Carlton and I discussed the possibility of adopting a child from a nearby children's home. We felt that by adopting this second child, we could help another family in need, and Ilisa would have a beloved sibling.

In Bolivia, the infrastructure of society is somewhat similar to American society in that when children are born to parents who can't afford to support them or provide food, shelter, and education, there are places like the Children's Home where these children are taken in. Sometimes the children return to their birth families, sometimes they're adopted into other loving families with the parents' consent, and other times they spend their entire lives up to adulthood under the care and supervision of the Children's Home. The Bolivian government does not support the Children's Home but people sponsor children and help by donating supplies.

We talked with Mrs. Stansberry, who was in charge of the Stansberry Children's Home located near where we lived. After a lot of thought, the day came when we gave her our final decision. "Yes," we said, "we would like to adopt and it does not matter to us if it is a girl or boy, but we would like a baby rather than an older child." Mrs. Stansberry said, "Wonderful. I'll let you know when a baby is available." We discussed what was involved with the adoption procedures and waited with excitement and anticipation.

I can still hear Mrs. Stansberry's voice over the phone when at last we received the call we'd been waiting for. "I'm calling to let you know a baby girl is available and you are welcome to come and see her. She is here in the Children's Home." I ran over to the office where Carlton was working to give him the news. "Guess what, a baby girl is available and we can go visit!" We were so excited and arranged to meet her that week.

This darling little girl was born on January 4, 1972, on her birth mother's birthday, at the Santa Cruz Hospital, in Bolivia.

Inside the Children's Home, we were led to the room just for babies, all well taken care of by the staff. Mrs. Stansberry said, "She is over along the window in the white crib." The very first sight of her brought tears of joy to my eyes and melted my heart. She laid there in her blue dress and looked so beautiful, with perfect features...and small ears. There was no way I could leave her, and in my heart I knew we would say, "Yes we would love to adopt her."

We named her Inez. Her birth mother, Angela, worked for a wealthy Bolivian family and the job helped Angela's family tremendously. Even so, Angela felt that the Stansberry Children's Home was essential to the health and well-being of her three children, whom she placed in their care. When Angela became pregnant with her fourth child, (Inez) she knew that this new child would also benefit from the aid of the Stansberry Children's Home, even before the child was born. Angela's oldest child moved to the country to live with relatives, and her other two children grew up in the Children's Home where they stayed until they were old enough to go out on their own as adults. If we hadn't adopted Inez, she most probably would have grown up in the Children's Home too.

I'm sure it was not easy for Inez's mother to give up raising her children. What I do know, is that we were two mothers making huge decisions in regard to a life we both considered precious.

When Carlton and I brought Inez home, Ilisa was excited and a wonderful sister to her right from the beginning. She was playful and eager to help whenever possible. It was always fun watching our two girls play together. We chose to name our daughter Inez, after a Bolivian woman we worked with whom we loved and respected. We had no idea until much later that when Inez was born, her mother had named her Angela after herself. We would have been happy to keep that name if we had known. As she grew older, we told Inez, "If you ever want to change your name back to Angela, please feel welcome to do so." Inez always kept the name we gave her, and it didn't seem to bother her but she knew we were fine if she ever decided to change it.

171

Through the years, we made sure we explained to Inez the full story of her adoption, and we visited her family in Bolivia twice. During the last visit, we met all of Inez's siblings as well as her birth mother, and it was a wondrous reunion. We sat around a long table eating the most delicious Bolivian meal and carried on our conversation in Spanish. We learned more details about her family that we hadn't known about before, and for the first time Inez met her oldest brother.

During the last visit, I said to Inez's mother, "Thank you for the gift of Inez, she brings us joy and so much love." She said, "Thank you for taking good care of her." The last visit was bittersweet. We had a wonderful time together, but realized we belonged to two very different worlds. Perhaps my history of blending my two worlds while growing up prepared me in some way for helping Inez deal with being a part of her two worlds. We are forever thankful for the good memories we made while visiting her birth family, and grateful for the time we have with each other as family.

When we returned to the States from Bolivia, we moved to Silver Springs, Maryland for a year. Carlton returned to his accounting job with Arthur Andersen in D.C. We now had our two children, and our lives were busy. I was with the girls 24/7 and living in the suburbs, which for me, was not the best place to live. I longed to be in the country. It took me a while to adjust to the traffic and the isolation of not knowing anyone. During this year I did a lot of soul searching because I found myself thinking so much about going to college. I enjoyed being a mother and did my best to find a balance but I was getting restless. Parenting, for me, was a full-time job and a big part of me felt I had to sacrifice my dreams and give to my family first. No doubt, this was residual from my own childhood, in which my mother dedicated herself entirely to her own family and the larger community without any freedom to entertain dreams of a career.

After living in Silver Springs, Maryland, we moved to Lancaster County, Pennsylvania, where Carlton was offered a wonderful job. We lived in Akron, Pennsylvania, for twenty-five years. We thought there were many advantages to living in a small town and it appealed to me better than the suburbs of Silver Springs. We were close to the grocery store, the park, and the community swimming pool. The elementary school was only a few blocks away so the girls walked to school. Raising the girls in Akron was quite different from both of our childhood experiences. We had to be creative about finding things to do with the girls.

I observed Inez's progress and kept a record of her achievements. She was a bright child and was right on target with what the books predicted for learning to walk and talk. She was a contented child and loved her big sister Ilisa, who often looked after her, and they spent a lot of time together. I remember the day Ilisa said, "Mom, Inez smiled and giggled while we were playing." And I said, "Good for you Ilisa, you are the first person who made her smile!" Inez did not smile for a long time, so this was a moment to celebrate!

One time I remember when Inez was outside playing she said, "I don't want to go barefoot—I don't like the feel of grass under my feet." I never understood why she felt that way, as I always loved going barefoot, but after that, I made sure she always had her shoes on. Our children develop in their own ways, and I am grateful for that in my own life and happy to support it in my children's lives.

The girls were gems and we had a lot of fun doing creative things together. In the winter, on snowy days, we'd go across the road from where we lived in a wooded area. I would say, "Girls, you wait here until I call you and then follow my tracks in the snow." It was our very own version of hide and seek. When they found me we'd make angels in the snow, by lying down and swooshing our arms and legs back and forth to make an impression that looked like an angel after we got up. They loved playing in the woods, building forts, and creating make-believe characters.

By the time the girls started school, I was looking forward to going to college even more—working with the guilt and yet determined to make my dream come true. I knew it would be a challenge and I felt ready to take it on. I applied at Millersville University, was accepted, and started my classes when the girls started theirs. This would be a long journey but I was willing to go for it. I went to school part-time during the day and had some evening classes thirty minutes from our house. I danced around the girls' schedule, Carlton's work, my now heavier load, and somehow we all managed. Ilisa and Inez became very close throughout their school years. Carlton, good father that he was, often read bedtime stories to the girls, played with them, and helped when I was away. As the girls got older, he loved playing basketball with them and they all enjoyed going on bike rides together.

Carlton and I have beautiful memories of when we went on family vacations, and how Ilisa and Inez were such great travelers on our road trips. They would content themselves in the backseat of our little car and be oh, so creative.

Ilisa did very well in school, and it wasn't long before we noticed her art skills. By the third grade, she was drawing and painting at an advanced level all by herself. I asked if she would like to take art lessons and she was very excited about the idea. All through her schooling, including college, she did beautiful artwork and won awards and worked hard to be successful. She played the violin for a few years but seemed to enjoy the creativity of art even more. In high school, Ilisa played field hockey and enjoyed running. She was so talented, and we were always happy to support her freedom to choose what she was interested in doing. In college, she majored in art, and after graduation, taught private art lessons, continued to do her own artwork, and developed a great reputation with collectors who enjoy buying it. We are so proud of her accomplishments, her positive spirit, and her giving heart.

During the summer months, the girls went to the community pool almost every day. This was a treat for many reasons. They learned to swim the proper way, and they had a chance to socialize with their friends. Games were offered, and of course, the snack bar was always a treat. This was very different from Mother's home cooking and trying to keep my head above water in the wild Susquehanna River when I was young!

Inez was more shy, quiet, and loved to read. She would rather read a book than eat when she was hungry. She, too, was blessed with talents such as singing and playing the flute and did very well in school. Inez asked one day, "May I join the high school band?" We said, "Sure if you can fit it into your busy schedule, that would be fine." Quite a contrast to my memories of sitting down at my desk, in tears, to await the finish of my group's parade around the classroom with their instruments! Inez always loved watching parades, so it was no surprise that she wanted to be in the band. We were very proud of her accomplishments. After her college years, she decided to move to California, worked for a few years, and then entered the police academy and became a police officer for the Los Angeles Police

Department. Who would have thought our quiet daughter would choose such an unforeseen path? As I write this story, she has achieved thirteen years of experience with the police department. How many people have benefitted from her assistance during that time? We feel very proud of her brave dedication to helping others in her community.

We have been so very fortunate to have our two beautiful daughters in our lives. We feel blessed and we believe that each one came into our lives for many reasons. Through all the joys and the tough times too, we have loved them and always wanted the best for them. Like most parents, we want our daughters to be happy, successful, and keep the faith. Their lives were so different from mine growing up, with all the do's and don'ts dangling in front of my face. I longed for my mother's patience and wisdom, but I felt I lacked her vast capacity for expressing those gifts sometimes. Amazingly we worked through the tough times and managed to carry on.

Being a mother taught me many lessons and the ones that I hold closest to my heart are loving my family unconditionally and keeping faith in them. Our daughters are now on their own journeys, and they are following paths of their own choosing. Carlton and I send love, light, and angels to both of them every day.

# Bolivian Adventure

*"We live in a wonderful world that is full of beauty,*
*charm and adventure. There is no end to the adventures*
*that we can have if only we seek them with our eyes open."*
~Jawaharlal Nehru

There were twelve of us, from different U.S. states and Canada, who went to Bolivia together, with a protestant organization called the Mennonite Central Committee to do volunteer work. Our group was composed of a great mix of professionals, including nurses, nutritionists, agriculturalists, teachers, and administrators. In total there were fifty workers assigned with the Mennonite Central Committee who worked along with the Peace Corps, other religious groups, and community leaders. Carlton was the assistant director, and I was the official hostess at the central headquarters for workers and visitors in Santa Cruz, Bolivia for two and a half years.

My husband and I were the only volunteers with a child in the group. Doubtful feelings crept in now and then as we asked each other, "What were we thinking bringing a brand new baby to this country?" As first-time parents, only twenty-three years old, we sometimes felt overwhelmed with keeping our daughter safe and healthy without the same amenities we had enjoyed in the U.S. As we adjusted, we discovered people were accommodating and supportive. They loved children. They were very helpful and patient as we tripped over our budding Spanish language skills as we learned to communicate with them.

We soon learned that Bolivia was one of the most beautiful countries to experience on the continent of South America. We had a chance to explore three different geographical areas in Bolivia. One of the most impressive places was the Highlands, where we could see the snow-capped Andes Mountains. When we got off of the plane in La Paz, we were at the highest capital in the world. The women there were often seen wearing their bright and colorful handwoven dresses and the men their alpaca ponchos. The soothing sound of the flute player while watching his sheep as we hiked near a village still plays in my mind. The lowlands were graced with palm trees, desert, and Florida-like weather. The tropical area was where the jungle was thick and the roads were more dangerous to drive than the busy L.A. freeways in the U.S. Here, the Amazon rainforest was, of course, characterized by rain—in some regions, 100 to 400 inches per year. There were different cultures in Bolivia, and the three official languages were Aymara, Quechua, and Spanish.

The Bolivian people taught us so much about the value of friends and family. We lived in Cochabamba with a Bolivian family for three months while attending Spanish classes. My taste buds still remember their fantastic Bolivian food. When one of the mothers asked the date of Ilisa's birthday, she said, "We must celebrate her first birthday, Bolivian style." They planned a huge party, made beautiful gifts, and served a colorful, decorative birthday cake. As our daughter learned to talk, she was soon speaking Spanish along with English. She often played with the Bolivian children who gave her a lot of attention.

Living in the city of Santa Cruz was a real adjustment since Carlton and I had both grown up in the quiet countryside of Pennsylvania. In Santa Cruz, the noise of traffic and loud street parties often felt invasive. The muddy roads, which at that time had no asphalt or stones, were a challenge for walking, driving, and cycling.

One day I remember feeling like a fly stuck in a web, with too much noise and too much city life surrounding me. I needed a break, and I longed to visit the rural Bolivian area called the *campo*. I had recently heard that the three Maryknoll Sisters from New York were planning to go to a village, near Cotoca, to distribute supplies after the rainy season. Even though I had a busy schedule, I decided to ask our director if I could go along to visit this village with the sisters, and he said, "Yes." I was so excited I started to do cartwheels in my mind. I made arrangements with

Carmen, our helper, to take care of our daughter, and my husband carried on my work while I was away.

We left early one morning before the intense sun extended her rays. Our driver arrived in a rusty old truck. I thought to myself, *I hope he brought his toolbox along. Looks like he might need it.* We would not see any gas stations; in fact, we would not be passing any services along the way during the whole trip.

In the back of the truck were stacks of feedbags, barrels of food, clothing, and four women. We sat on top of the bags, Bolivian style, and traveled into a very thick jungle-like area. Tall palm trees, weeds, and thick brush covered our invisible roadway. On several occasions, the driver's assistant got out of the truck and used his machete to clear the brush and high weeds. One thing I knew for sure—I was on the ride of my life, and it was nothing like the back of the truck with my family on moving day all those years ago.

Earlier, I had been told that it would take approximately eight hours to get to this village. I soon realized this would not be an ordinary trip. If we had to go to the bathroom, we needed to get off and go near the truck, outdoors with no facilities. *Yeah right,* I thought to myself as I crossed my legs. I also heard about the snakes and giant tarantulas that came out at night. I learned quickly: you do what you have to do. So when one of the nuns got off of the truck to relieve herself, I followed, and like cats and dogs, we marked our spots.

About five hours into our trip, one of the nuns announced we were low on water. One of the sisters recommended we stop at the next puddle to collect water for cooking. I hid my surprise and trusted that they knew what they were doing. They had lived in Bolivia for years and had made this trip many times. Sure enough, when we came to the next water puddle, we gathered it up, boiled it for cooking, and used it for drinking and to make dinner.

The scene of entering that beautiful village is so vivid, as though it happened yesterday. We received a warm welcome from the people as they all lined up to greet us.

Their houses were covered with thatched roofs and surrounded by wooden posts. There were open fire pits for cooking, and simple wooden toys scattered on the ground that were handmade for the children. I heard the noise of cackling chickens and saw many dogs that looked very frail.

They had built showers outside under the sky for gringos who came for a visit. These shelters were made of lightweight wood, each with a shiny silver bucket of water hanging inside. A nail was fixed in the bottom of the bucket such that when you pushed the nail up, the water slowly trickled out. That was the first time I took a shower under the stars. It seemed surreal, but I loved every minute, out in nature and the country.

We slept in swaying hammocks, with mosquito netting draped over the top. It now dawned on me why we had to have so many shots, especially for preventing malaria. I realized for the first time in my life how different life was for people in rural Bolivia from what I was used to. At that moment I felt very thankful for what I had. I never wanted to take the amenities of our life for granted again.

My memories of that experience will follow me forever, like music replaying in my mind. The images are so vivid of the people who lived life differently, who were so friendly and appreciative. They were eager to show us their homes, their gardens, their artwork, and invited us to share their food. Maybe I wasn't always up to drinking their famous beverage called *chicha*, a fermented drink derived from corn, but out of politeness, I managed. If you like the taste of Vicks' cough syrup, you would probably like *chicha*.

Visiting that serene village of beautiful people gave me a broader perspective of life in another part of the world. I was like a sponge taking in every detail. Spending several days with three of the happiest people I'd ever met, the nuns, listening to them sing, tell jokes, and share their stories was better than watching any TV show I had ever experienced, even the worldly ones. The nuns respectfully blended with the Bolivian people with love and compassion, showing genuine dedication to their work. They had no idea that the inspiration they showered on me was a lifelong gift.

When I returned to my duties back in Santa Cruz, I rambled on like a child, talking non-stop about my adventures, as my husband listened intently. The trip had enriched my life forever.

I will always treasure the memories of Bolivia; it was such an adventure, seeing this land of contrast and beauty. It was a place where people have similar likes, basic needs, and interests like ours, but their lives and culture were quite different. My mind was stretched wide like a sunrise, and my life was transformed. I learned the profound lesson that all people, no matter where we live, no matter what culture we come from, are connected.

# Road Trip to the Chapare

*"Adventure is worthwhile in itself."* -Amelia Earhart

When we lived in Bolivia from 1969 to 1972 doing volunteer work, we traveled to some beautiful and dangerous places throughout the country. One particular time, we were invited to go to the Chapare, leaving from the city of Cochabamba, to visit some of the volunteers who worked in agriculture. A friend asked, "You are going where?" "Yes, we're going to the Chapare, called Villa Tunari, for a visit," I replied. He just smiled as though he knew something we didn't. He said, "Have a safe trip and say hello to the volunteers for me."

Many volunteers were isolated from the cities sometimes for months, in places where it felt like time stood still. So they appreciated visitors, especially those living in remote areas like the Chapare. As the assistant directors of the volunteer program, we felt it important to visit the volunteers.

The trip took eight hours by bus over dirt roads with potholes, and there were no guardrails on those precipitous mountain roads! Many families with young children and babies took this bus trip every day because it was the only road from Cochabamba in the mountains to the lush jungle lowlands. "Why would people take this trip?" I asked. "Sometimes it was to visit family, buy food to bring back and sell, or to work there," a Bolivian told me.

The Chapare region is on the eastern side, between the high Andes mountains and the upper Amazon basin, an area of steep, jungle-covered mountains where the roads twist around the high peaks and mountain lakes, then drop steeply into deep, steaming tropical valleys. Most of the territory consists of valley rainforests that surround the area's main waterway, the Chapare River.

Traveling by bus was very common in Bolivia, especially to go anywhere outside of the cities. I often traveled by bus alone in the city so I didn't have any second thoughts. HA! Carlton and I were young and full of adventure, but we had no idea what this trip would be like! As we approached the bus station, we noticed the bus was well worn with many rusty spots and dents here and there on both sides. The tires? *Have faith,* I thought to myself. The friendly bus driver welcomed us onto the bus, and we found our seats. Many people wearing their colorful clothing and carrying rainbow-colored woven blankets were getting on with their children, chickens, and did I see a small sheep? This bus was packed!

On this particular road, the Province had a system that all vehicles were to travel one way into the Chapare on certain days and one way out on other days. If anyone decided not to follow this system it put many people in jeopardy. The drivers would have to figure out how to pass each other on a very narrow road while looking over a 2,000-foot cliff on the one side. The risk of traveling in any vehicle on this road was very high because the road was narrow and had many drop-offs to the valley below.

This road in Bolivia was known as "Death Road" and continues to be one of the most dangerous roads in the world. Just looking at internet photos of it can give your stomach the willies, but we didn't know that when we got onto the bus to head out.

That was another piece of information we didn't know about at that time. As we began the journey towards snow peaked mountains, it was hard to imagine we were headed for the forest and jungle area below. Along the way, we saw many crosses adorned with artificial flowers, in memory of those who had died along this road. Many vehicles went over the cliffs each year due to bad weather, a drunk driver, or trying to pass another vehicle. Buses and trucks were used on this road to deliver supplies and to take people to visit friends or to work. It wasn't unusual to see people riding outside on top of the vehicles with their supplies such as fruit, vegetables, and livestock.

We started out on our journey with excitement. The Bolivian people were amiable. I remember feeling excited to make this trip. Carlton and

I were in awe of the beautiful, snow-covered mountains. This experience was an excellent opportunity to see something different and meet new people. A few hours into the trip we had to stop several times to have something fixed. The driver smiled as though it was no big deal. He got his rusty toolbox from under the seat and used his tools to fix the problem. Fortunately, the issues were not major, and he knew how to deal with them.

As the road snaked around bend after bend, children and some adults got sick and were throwing up. From time to time we had a bathroom stop, no, not like a rest area in the U.S. This was right outside the bus under the heavens. The men went on one side of the bus and the women on the other, and we all took care of business. Talk about letting go of our inhibitions! And yes, this was why we were advised to carry paper at all times.

Fortunately, Carlton and I did not get sick, but the smells were overwhelming, and I remember having to cover my nose. We had several hours to go, and I just wanted to sleep, yes SLEEP. With constant noise like the outcry from a child, the eruption of danger ahead, the clanging bell around an animal's neck or the bus driver suddenly stomping on his brakes, sleep was not an option!

After our eight-hour trip, Carlton and I were more than happy to get off the bus and touch our feet to solid ground! We were thrilled to reach our destination safely, but I'm sure we looked like wilted flowers. One of the volunteers came to meet us at the bus stop and invited us to his house. He asked, "So, how was your trip?" and we said, "It was certainly an adventure we never experienced before!" He gave us a warm welcome and had the most delicious meal prepared for us to top it off! By now we were hungry since we ate very little on the bus trip. Homemade vegetable soup and homemade bread were just the beginning of his delicious meal. He proudly told us that he grew everything nearby.

In the Chapare, it rains year-round, and they can receive up to 400 inches a year. It rained the two days we were there, and at night, as we listened to the sound of the rain on the roof, it didn't take us long to fall asleep. This place was peaceful, and the rain seemed to wash away our worries. The lush plants and the jungle are the most beautiful sight to observe. The rain brings out the best colors and shades of green. I asked the volunteer, "Did I hear a monkey in the distance?" He said, "Yes, there are many here." I loved watching monkeys and couldn't wait until the next day to see them flying from tree to tree.

The volunteers who worked in this area were single men, and they helped in the community teaching the local farmers how to raise different crops and ways to increase the yields of their crops. Potatoes were grown in the highlands, but here in the Chapare, they raised a variety of vegetables and fruits such as corn, soybeans, sugar, melons, mangos, papayas, bananas and coffee. We had fresh juices each morning and tea, or *café con leche*. The *café* made my hair stand up. If you like STRONG coffee you would be in heaven.

Our trip was an adventure, and I'm glad I didn't know all the facts beforehand about the dangers or I probably would not have gone. I'm so happy we took the risk and were open to learning new things about the Bolivian culture. Thankfully we had a safe return, and we made many beautiful memories to take back with us. I was reminded not to take things for granted. I can still see the beautiful and kind people on the bus trip. It was one of the most unforgettable trips I have ever taken.

# Mother's Courageous Spirit

*"All you need is the plan, the road map, and the courage to press on to your destination." -*Earl Nightingale

Bolivia, South America, was, to me, a land of contrast, beautiful people, delicious food, and a slower pace of life. Carlton and I had been living there for over two years and it was certainly an adventure. We loved the culture and learned so much from the people. Our oldest daughter was now two years old and we had just adopted our second daughter from the Children's Home nearby. Life was exciting, and we realized our Bolivian adventure would soon come to a close as we started making plans to return to the states.

Earlier in the year, my father died and my mother was now living alone in Pennsylvania. One day I asked Carlton, "Why don't we invite my mother to come down for a visit?" I thought she would love the adventure, though I knew that she had never traveled outside the U.S., and it would be a stretch for her to consider visiting Bolivia. Carlton was in favor and we both agreed she might really enjoy the culture, sightseeing, and spending time with our girls.

So one day I wrote her a nice long letter. "Dear Mother, Greetings from Bolivia." We wrote to each other almost each week. I explained that Carlton and I would love for her to come for a visit. We were informed of another couple coming to Bolivia and they could meet in Florida and travel together from there. They were willing to help her get to Bolivia. Mother was a very faithful writer and after the invitation I was so eager to receive her mail. Mother was never the impulsive type and with this decision she

187

had to think it through, pray about it, and make sure the family at home was comfortable with her coming. Finally with the third letter, she sent a precious, simple poem she'd written, saying that she had decided to come!

I was so excited for many reasons. Most of my memories of my mother were of her working on the farm, being there for us children and helping others. I was so excited because this was a once in a lifetime experience for her.

The much anticipated day finally came when she was scheduled to arrive in Bolivia. We met her at the Santa Cruz Airport with huge smiles and countless hugs. It was so great to see her again! "Do you have more luggage to pick up?" we asked, as we saw that she carried her one and only suitcase with her. "No thank you," she said, "I'll only be here for a few weeks so I really don't need much." That was Mother, keeping things simple. She always knew how to travel light!

When she walked into our house, she met our daughters with open arms. They were thrilled to see her. Carmen, our maid, was also delighted to meet her and gave her a warm welcome, so much a part of the Bolivian culture.

We planned the days' adventures, and during the last weeks, a visit with the people in the *campo*—the Bolivian term for rural area. We lived near the city and we wanted her to see the contrasts. We lived very comfortably whereas most of the volunteers lived and worked in the country, as teachers, agriculturalists, and nurses, in very simple housing. When we got settled, one of the first things we did was take Mother to the open market in Santa Cruz. It certainly was different from shopping at our U.S. grocery stores where everything was packaged and lined up on shelves, and the wheeled grocery carts just waited for us to load them up. In the open market the food items were piled loosely in baskets and spread out upon tables and blankets in the open air, and we could smell the fragrance of the fruits and spices, basketry, and hand woven textiles. I could tell she was like a sponge, taking everything in. I was so proud of her and realized how courageous she always was! I said, "Mother, you are in Bolivia!" and we both giggled. It was fun seeing her in a different light and more free. When we got home from the market I explained how everything had to be washed in iodine. We were very careful with how we prepared food, in order to avoid coming down with amoebic dysentery or hepatitis.

By the second week of her stay we planned a trip to the country to visit some of the volunteer teachers and people who worked in public health and agriculture. By truck we drove over bumpy dirt roads. The sights were quite a contrast to even the most rural parts of Pennsylvania, which my mother was used to. She would point out how beautiful the landscapes were and was impressed by how hard the women worked. No washers or dryers, all the washing was done by hand. On a very deep level my mother could relate and empathize, because she knew what hard work was like.

Whenever volunteers arrived at a village, the first thing they did was inquire what the people needed help with and together they worked out a plan. They made a list of things to do. For example, in this village in the *campo*, there was no running water, so they planned to dig a well, creating a huge reservoir so people could come and collect the water to take to their homes. If there were no schools, the volunteers and the village people designed and built a school. The whole idea was to work together to help people help themselves. My mother was in awe and couldn't believe how simply the Bolivian people lived in these rural areas. During the 1970s, while we lived there, these people in the country did not have radios or TVs. Their lives were as different as day and night compared to those who lived in the city.

A real highlight for us, of course, was to enjoy the Bolivian food, especially their homemade bread. It was to die for! They built their own open clay ovens where the bread was baked and it was always served fresh each morning. It was good for us to be exposed to this different way of life.

When we returned to our home in the city, we were exhausted, but Carmen had things under control. She was so competent and loving in helping us take care of the household duties as well as spending time with Ilisa and Inez. We were so blessed to have Carmen with us.

The next big adventure was to take my mother to a city called, Sucre, the constitutional capital of Bolivia. We made arrangements with a pilot to take us there. He told us he was experienced and had flown for many years, as he probably noticed our anxious looks. I can still see my mother not totally relaxed flying in that tiny plane, but she was brave and didn't complain. She prayed for Divine protection and trusted that all would be well. The pilot showed us different landmarks, as his wife sat beside him knitting away. I asked him at one point, if we had to make an emergency landing where would we go? Slowly he flew lower and showed us small areas of sandy patches along the riverbed. He pointed and said, "Right down there on the sand," as my knuckles began to sweat. Mother and I looked at each other nervously giggling, and she asked, "Are we soon there?" HA! I'm guessing he had his toolbox with him too, and knew just how to use those tools to good advantage.

We finally arrived and landed at a small airport near the city. We made arrangements to stay in Sucre for a few days, so the first thing we did was find our hotel. I remember the place looked rather drab, with cement floors, dim lights, and our rooms felt very cold. We did our best to adjust and drank tea to get warm. First we toured the city for few hours and then decided to return to the hotel and go to bed early because the next day was packed with places to go and things to see.

There are many kinds of museums in Sucre; everything from exhibits about the processing of silver, gold, and precious gems, to the production of textiles. Sucre has an abundance of art galleries, and cathedrals and architecturally beautiful buildings line the streets. My mother took it all in and sometimes was overwhelmed with the magnitude of treasures.

We walked inside and sat in several different cathedrals and my mother was touched with the number of people who came for mass or to sit and meditate. This was another big contrast to her experiences back home. These places of worship with gold and ornate decor compared to the plain looking churches that she attended back home were wondrous for her to experience.

It was a gift for me to see my mother in a different light on this visit. She never judged or complained about the things she might not agree with. It was refreshing to see her literally in another world appreciating the differences. So often I did not have the opportunity to see this while growing up, as she was as much confined by the rules of the stringent head of our family as I was. So many things were pointed out as being wrong or unacceptable during those times, so to see her just taking all of this in and enjoying the moments was delightful.

After three days visiting Sucre we returned to our home in Santa Cruz. We had a lot to talk about and were delighted that all had gone well. We had one more week until it was time to return to the U.S. Carlton and I had plenty to do, what with packing and saying our farewells. The moments were bittersweet knowing that we were leaving Bolivia.

I learned from Mother's special visit that she was more courageous than many women her age. When we returned to the U.S. it seemed like she was just getting started in her discovery of new adventures. Her travels continued and she certainly left a legacy for all of us in the family. My mother was a shining star no matter where she left her imprints. I admire how she lived a courageous life and I would love to follow her path.

# Finding My Way in a City

*"It is not the destination where you end up but the mishaps and memories you create along the way!"* ~Penelope Riley

After we settled in at home, back in the U.S. for a time, I was ready for another adventure. I was feeling over the top with excitement to take the train to Philadelphia from Lancaster. I had arranged to attend an art workshop for the weekend at the Art Institute. I was prepared to go by myself but felt anxious because I usually had someone with me whenever I traveled.

Our girls were in elementary school at the time, and I had to make sure babysitters were lined up, and things were in order at home before I left.

Babysitters, check. Meals, check, oh that's right Carlton liked to make lots of macaroni and cheese whenever I had to travel, so no worries, he was good at that. I finished packing and made sure I had my tickets, itinerary, and the reservation where I had arranged to stay. On my paper, there were four places suggested for lodging. It looked like there was a familiar "chain hotel" not far from the workshop. I figured it would be similar to the one in Lancaster that I was familiar with, so that is where I made my reservation. Think again!

The trip to Philadelphia went fast, probably because I sat beside an exciting lady who loved to talk like I did. We chatted a lot about our travels and families. We arrived in Philadelphia as scheduled. I decided, since I had luggage, to go directly to the hotel and go to the Art Institute the next morning to register.

Upon arrival at the hotel, my first impression was *This is a noisy place!* I signed in at the front desk, and the lady explained where my room was located. I thanked her and went to find the elevator. There it was, plastered with a big sign that said, Broken. The rugged, dirty stairway was around the corner. As I dragged my suitcase up the stairway to the second floor, the noise got louder and louder. Kids were crying, adults were yelling, and the place was filthy. The aroma of burnt toast and cigarettes sailed through the hallway. I soon felt very uncomfortable and decided I could not stay. I quickly went back down the broken steps to the desk and canceled my reservation without any discussion. May I assume this lady was just glad for a job and didn't care about how the place looked?

I rooted through my purse to dig out my itinerary to see if I could find another place, like a real hotel. Yes, a few blocks from this hotel was another one, though not part of that familiar chain. I decided to check it out, after all, it was on the list. I was getting anxious because dusk was creeping in and I was not feeling safe on this street, lined by a row of dingy bars and glowing with shiny red lights on the buildings in-between. I was nervously chuckling to myself and thinking, *What did I get myself into?* Finally, I crossed the street and walked into the dimly lit hotel. A short white-haired man, barely 5 feet tall, with a mustache, came to the window and asked if he could help me. If he only knew! I asked in a low voice, "Is it safe for me to stay here?" and he looked around and said, "Of course." A stupid question on my part! My intuition already told me I should not be there, but I didn't want to walk the streets alone in the dark to look for yet another place.

I decided to stay but was a nervous wreck as I heard two drunks yelling and fighting outside the building. I went into the hallway to use the pay phone to call my husband to let him know where I was staying. I told him I felt like I was taking a risk staying at this place but was afraid to go out in the dark to look for another place, and I didn't have extra money for a taxi. He said, "I wish I could help, but at least I know where you are staying." I said, "I'll manage, I'm just not used to being in the city by myself." It was my choice to take this adventure, so I had to keep the faith and hope for the best.

I slowly crept up to the front desk again where the little man was waiting to tell me my room number. He said, "Your room number is 203, and it's on the second floor with a shared bathroom." Sweet Rosemary, I forgot to check before I made reservations; a shared bathroom at this place would not work. He might as well have said the room number was 666! I climbed the stairs, and I soon realized I was a minority in the building and a country girl to boot. There it was, Room 203 with the number 3 dangling off its hinge. I stared at the chipped white paint on the door and entered, only to be greeted with disgusting, stale cigarette smoke stench, and filth.

My imagination was running wild thinking about what could be crawling on the floor and walls, never mind the bed linens. The first thing I did was lock the door but that didn't instill much confidence. As I looked around the room, I noticed the cracked window near my bed and just outside was a fire escape. Yes, fire escapes were useful, but in this case, I felt that anyone could step right from that staircase straight into my bed. The filthy, torn curtains barely closed. Every table had mounds of dust, and the floor felt sticky. I was afraid to lift the covers, let alone sleep in the bed.

I urgently had to go to the bathroom, *Yeah right, give me a truck and a nun and a jungle any day!* There was no way I was going to walk down that hallway to the public bathroom. I found a paper cup and peed away, no, make that two paper cups. I tried to pull myself together and took a simple sponge bath; funny how I remember my mother doing the same thing, though she didn't have to, with the wonderful amenities of her home. I decided I'd go to bed early so that I could get up early and make a quick dash from this place. So I laid on the bed overtop the covers, as stiff as a board, besieged by the overwhelming noise, which got even louder because of the increasing infestation of intoxicated people who were out on the street.

I slept fitfully that night and was ever so happy to see the light through the cracked window the next morning. I quickly gathered my belongings, had another quick sponge bath, and swiftly brushed my teeth. I left in a hurry, taking my courage with me.

When I arrived at the Art Institute, there was a long line of people waiting to register. As I got in line, I had to chuckle to myself because I didn't see too many people with suitcases. While waiting in line, I turned around, and there was a lady in white bobby socks and sneakers, dressed casually, who was also alone. I soon introduced myself, and she told me her name. With a strong Southern accent, she said, "I'm Helen from North Carolina." I smiled and serenely asked her where she was staying for the weekend and she said, "At Temple University in the dorms." I said, "Really? That place wasn't listed on my paper," and then I spewed out my story, not so serenely. She said, "Well honey, you stick with me, and I'll help you find a place where I'm staying." She had no idea how relieved I was. She took me under her wing like a mother hen. We registered, had coffee, and then attended the first meeting.

After the meeting, she said, "We have plenty of time until the next session, let's book it back to the university and find a place for you to stay." "Wonderful," I said, and we took off. I giggled to myself because Helen was a fast walker and knew exactly where she was going. I loved it because I no longer was in charge. We got to the office, and sure enough, there was a room available near hers on the same floor. She had no idea how grateful I was for her help, though I thanked her profusely.

My weekend was like a whirlwind, and one I'll never forget. Being courageous is a good thing. Learning how to deal with challenges is another good thing. Life can be unpredictable. Better planning would have been helpful; definitely I would remember it for the next time. What I always find fascinating is how people show up just when I need them. Helen became my earth angel and friend, and that was surely heaven sent.

# Great Expectations

*"When you have expectations, you are setting yourself up*
*for disappointment." ~Ryan Reynolds*

Our daughters were 11 and 13 years old when I got my next big brainstorm. "It's time we take a trip out West," I declared to my husband one day. I thought it would be great to show our girls what it's like to travel across the U.S. by car. I said, "You can't really comprehend the vastness of geography when you study it in school." I wanted them to see and feel the contrasts and notice how each state has its unique culture and natural beauty. It sure sounded good to me.

My husband and I had already traveled to the West Coast several times, which made it easier for us to decide when it came time to bring our children on such a trip. We planned, packed, and during the summer of 1981, we filled the trunk of our red Super Beetle VW so full the latch barely shut. Our daughters sat in the back seat with their games, puffy pillows, and books. It was close quarters for our family, like being stuffed together inside a sardine can.

I made sure we had a list of travel games, like Road Trip Bingo and The License Plate Game, to name a couple. Singing was a hit and the girls loved entertaining us by singing the new songs they had learned at summer camp, like "Watermelon, Watermelon," "Baby Bumble Bee," and "Peanut Butter and Jelly."

We were enjoying ourselves until we hit Texas, where it was 100-plus degrees and our red Beetle did not have air conditioning. We kept wiping the sweat off our faces as we cruised west on Interstate 40. The windows were open but the air felt like a blast of heat from a hot oven. "Texas might be unique for its heat and dust but I would never want to live here," declared our youngest daughter. "I know," I said, "we need a pool, shade, or some ice to cool us off."

"Let's look for a rest stop and take a break," I said, as I wondered which was worse, hot air blowing in our faces or walking next to the car with the heat radiating off the pavement beneath our feet. When we stopped to stretch our legs, we drank lots of water and poured some over our heads to refresh ourselves. After a few more complaints about the unbearable heat, we managed to drag ourselves back into the car and continued on our way.

Thank God children have great imaginations! It wasn't long before our daughters decided to present their version of the NPR radio program called "All Things Considered," in the heat. My husband and I cracked up laughing as they interviewed Mrs. Snellwiser whom they introduced as an author who wrote mystery novels. They asked her questions like, "When did you become interested in writing mysteries?" and "Do you prefer writing in an air-conditioned room or one with the windows wide open to let the heat in?" I soon interrupted and announced, "Cheers, we are now in Arizona!" My excitement was not subtle. I was so excited to see their reaction to the glorious, mammoth sight of the Grand Canyon!

We parked at the South Rim. As we eagerly jumped out of the car and walked around, my husband and I started to explain, "This gorge is over 200 miles long and there are several hiking trails that go all the way to the bottom. Many people go whitewater rafting in the Colorado River, far below." We were so excited to see this amazing place again but soon noticed the girls were not impressed. Our older daughter said, "Is this it? I'm ready to go."

My heart sank to my toes, and I felt disappointed, realizing that this was not the hit I had imagined it would be. Isn't that sometimes how it is when we do things with other people, especially those who are much younger than we are? I had started out with the best of intentions. We made good memories and our trip was certainly an adventure. But, I had to ask myself, *Were my expectations too high?*

I learned an important life lesson for myself on that trip: Don't expect others to enjoy the same things that I do.

# Unstoppable

*"Life is ten percent what you experience and ninety percent how you respond to it."* ~Dorothy M. Neddermeyer

On a beautiful August day during the late 1990s, my husband and I set out with our daughter on a train trip to New York City. Inez was meeting a friend to travel to Spain and had invited us to go along to see her off. Carlton and I loved traveling by train and had taken this trip from Lancaster to Philadelphia and on to New York many times. We laughed as we struggled onto the train in Lancaster with our tower of luggage. We eased into our seats and soon were on our way. We talked non-stop and had fun catching up on family news. Now that Inez was living in California, this special time together was a gift.

Before we knew it, the train was making its scheduled stop at 30th Street Station in Philadelphia, one of the busiest rail stations in the country. We heard the announcement that passengers had fifteen minutes before the train would depart for New York City.

To my surprise, Inez said, "I think I want to get off and buy something to drink."

Carlton said, "I'll go with you."

"Really, is it necessary?" I asked.

My husband assured me, "We'll be right back."

I was not thrilled because we had a lot of luggage, but I said, "Okay, go ahead. I'll watch our things."

They took off in a hurry.

While I waited, I noticed that most of the other passengers had also stepped outside for a smoke or just to stretch. Our seats were near the door, so I decided I would also get off for a little fresh air. In less than ten minutes, those of us who had been standing outside hopped back on and took our seats. Suddenly, I noticed the train was moving. At first I thought it was backing up to change tracks as trains often do at main stations. Then my heart did a flip! I realized the train was not changing tracks but going forward. My husband and daughter had not returned. There was no way fifteen minutes had gone by. I felt a panic attack coming over me.

I began speaking loudly, "My husband and daughter are not on the train!" I stood up and asked, "What should I do?"

What a revelation! No one paid any attention to me. The other passengers were back in their seats reading or talking among themselves, acting as if they were stone deaf. Apparently I was on my own.

I decided to take a risk and go after the conductor who was collecting tickets in the next car. I ran through the connecting doorway yelling to the conductor, "I need help! Stop the train! My husband and daughter didn't get back on." Some people in this car did lower their newspapers and glance at me. They appeared to be thinking, *Who is this crazy woman?*

The conductor slowly came toward me and said, "Lady, that is their problem."

I couldn't believe what I heard. "You can't help me?" I asked.

"No. Go sit down."

I went back to my seat sobbing like a frightened child. I was on my way to New York City without my husband and daughter. I knew I would be fine, but I was worried about the mountain of luggage. What would I do when I arrived at Penn Station? I imagined myself being a great target for someone to snatch our things. I was alone with more than I could handle.

After a good cry, I gathered my wits, took out my cell phone and called my husband. "You missed the train, and I'm on my way to New York City by myself."

He said in his calm voice, "We'll figure it out. Hold tight."

After hanging up, I remembered I had the customer service number for Amtrak in my purse. I quickly found it and called. "Sir," I said, "I'm on the train from Philadelphia to New York City. In Philadelphia, we were told we had fifteen minutes before the train left for New York City. My husband

and daughter got off to get something to drink. About ten minutes later, before they had returned, the train pulled out. When I yelled for help, the conductor told me to go sit down and said that it was our problem."

"You didn't get any help from the conductor?"

"No, and I would like to know when my husband and daughter can catch the next train."

He said, "Hmmm, I'll call the station and see what I can do." I was very relieved and thanked him several times.

With that, my emotions changed. I stopped sobbing and starting laughing hysterically. I called my sisters and told them I was on a runaway train. We were all laughing, but I was still very uncomfortable with the situation.

The conductor appeared in our car to collect tickets. He came to my seat and noticed I was still upset. He saw the mountain of luggage and asked if I wanted a "redcap." I'm thinking "nightcap," and said, "Yes, I could use one right about now."

He said, "Someone will meet you at the station in New York to help with your luggage." I almost jumped for joy, but there was no way I was going to let this man see my happiness. I thanked him, but could I trust him? He was the person who had rudely said he could not help me.

Within minutes of my arrival in New York City, a short, friendly guy came up to me and asked, "Are you the lady who needs help with the luggage?"

"Yes, I really appreciate you being here," I said. I told him what had happened in Philadelphia.

"Lady," he said, "this happens more often than you'd think, for reasons beyond our control, where they leave Philadelphia before the time you think they will."

"There is something wrong with this picture," I replied, and thought to myself, *Maybe this whole thing is a scam so "redcaps" can earn extra money.*

Mr. Redcap walked with me into the station and said, "We'll wait here in the center so we can see people when they get off the trains."

Sure enough, within minutes Carlton and Inez appeared. What a relief. They had managed to get on the next train, which departed soon after the one I was on. We tipped Mr. Redcap, who smiled from ear to ear.

Whether this was a scam or not, I appreciated Redcap's assistance. I have found that life is always full of twists and turns. What I know for sure is that speed is essential when time is of the essence, and sometimes that means things are unstoppable!

# Being a Nontraditional Student

*"The biggest adventure you can take is to live the life of your dreams."* ~Oprah Winfrey

I had hung onto my dream of being a teacher for a very long time. Finally I decided it was now or never. This era was the start of nontraditional students returning to college, and I was one of the first. I was so excited because I never gave up my desire to get an education. Even though having a family and going to school at the same time would be a risk and a challenge, I pressed forward. For some reason, age was not a deciding factor for me when I made my decision. I felt that if I could still do my share at home with our family, and accomplish my personal goals as well, I could give myself permission to manage both. My husband often said, "Go for it, I know you can do it." He was very supportive, along with my friends who cheered me on. I felt comfortable moving forward.

I'd had many experiences in the working world, and I knew what I didn't want to do for a career. I was not excited about sitting in an office all day, shuffling papers and answering the phone. I wanted to be more active.

College is not for everyone, but I wanted the experience and education, and to prove to myself that I could accomplish my goals. I didn't mind if I was a late bloomer; this was the path I chose. I was motivated now, and despite any negative messages from the past, I remained steadfast. I was the only girl in my family who went to college. That being said, it wasn't that we couldn't go; it was a choice that each of us could make. We all chose our pathways as we grew older and left the farm, and we each chose the path that felt right to us. My inner voice spoke loudly! I knew within my heart to follow my dreams of becoming a teacher.

There was no doubt in my mind that I was eager and ready to go to college. I was prepared to focus, and I knew what I wanted for my future career. I was less intimidated because I had already experienced many adventures in the world, like living in Bolivia for two and a half years. When I began classes, I found the younger students were very supportive and fun to be around. For me, college was a place worth attending, and I thrived on learning new things. I was very organized and managed my time the best I could. I also knew that I wanted to pay for my own education and I believed it was a good investment. Balancing family, a part-time job, and studies sometimes put me into a whirlwind, but I was determined. Yes, sometimes there were sacrifices made for my family and myself, but I never gave up.

My very first college course was speech class, which was fitting for me because I loved to talk. I was happy to present every speech although being critiqued wasn't always enjoyable. I was now in a different world taking courses with a diverse group of younger students. I was there because I wanted to be, while some were dragging their feet and were not as motivated. I thrived on learning new things, and I felt content.

Most of my professors were helpful and accepted me as a non-traditional student. However, a few were challenged because this was a new experience for them as well. For example, one day I asked if I could bring my daughters to class when they didn't have school and I couldn't get a babysitter lined up. I was fortunate because the professors had no problem with them coming along. Our girls were in grade school at the time and didn't seem to mind coming with me. They seemed to enjoy the adventure far more than they'd enjoyed the Grand Canyon. It gave them the opportunity to see what it took to balance the facets of my life; I was more than just "Mother" to them.

I believed in being on time for my classes. My daughters can vouch for that. I always encouraged them to be ready, and bring something along to do when they came with me. I was often the first student to arrive for each class, and the others slowly trickled in through the door. We still laugh about me having to be on time, as we often had to sit and wait for the class to begin. Being able to choose a seat in the front row was important to me so that I could really pay attention to my teachers. Today my daughters tease me whenever I take a workshop or class, saying, "So Mom, were you on time and did you sit in the front row?" HA! "Of course!"

Naturally, every course was different and some easier than others. As I paced myself through one class and another, I had many thoughts about what I wanted to teach. I always loved social studies, history, and biology. As I was getting my basic courses finished, I realized I had to take art, physical education, and music classes. I thought I could just breeze through these courses. I signed up for swimming and badminton only to learn that badminton was very competitive and we played co-ed. I managed, but being short, there was just so much I could do, and I worked hard to be quick and stay focused. I had never played "power badminton" before!

My swimming class was hilarious because I only knew a few basics, like how to tread water so you don't drown in wild river currents, but by the end of the course, I had successfully learned how to swim. Often, when we raced competitively, our team won, being the fastest against the other team, which made me feel great. Having to jump off the high dive at twenty-nine years old felt like diving out of an airplane, although I never actually had that experience; I could only imagine! Heights were never something I enjoyed, but I managed to accomplish what was required.

Taking a music class was a real joy. The professor made it enjoyable by having us engage in the music and sharing stories about the many musicians. I felt so sad when he announced that he had cancer, but said he was determined to teach as long as he could. I was always impressed by his positive attitude. He left an impression on me—never to give up!

My art classes were a real eye-opener for me. My art background was limited, but I found the courses so interesting. I loved art history, and learning how to use all the different art media. I was like a sponge absorbing new techniques in the arts. My classes were sometimes challenging, but they forced me out of my comfort zone, and I found myself enjoying them immensely. This was when I became excited about teaching art. Soon I made the decision to major in art education because I thought it would be lots of fun to teach students and help them to express their creativity.

Though I wasn't encouraged to dabble in the art world while growing up, being creative was a big part of my life. We didn't have an overabundance of things, and there was always plenty of work, with which we were always encouraged to be creative. I created my own world many times while living in the restricted community of my childhood. I imagined being many things while growing up, but the one dream that really stuck with me was teaching. Envisioning myself teaching art and encouraging others to be creative felt exciting.

The sun seemed to shine brighter than ever, on Graduation Day at Millersville University. What a joy to have Carlton, our daughters, my mother, siblings, and friends attend. I can still hear my older brother shouting in celebration when it was my turn to receive my diploma. I felt blessed and thankful and ready to move on.

The joy of following my dream, going to college, teaching, and later getting my Master's degree was hard work, but it was all worth it. Somehow I didn't miss a beat. With the help and support of my family, friends, and the Divine, I prevailed. The path I took was a huge risk maybe, at that time—it was the road less traveled, but I found it worthwhile to the end.

# Black and White Photography

*"It is during our darkest moments that we must focus to see the light."* -Aristotle Onassis

One of my favorite classes in college was photography. I thought, *finally I can use my new Canon camera.* The professor was excellent for explaining its history and teaching us how to process our black and white photos. Black and white photography is an art form. Unless they were enhanced by hand, all photos were black and white until the mid-20th century when color photography evolved. I was in my glory doing the assignments.

I loved when we were asked to make a pinhole camera, with which I captured unique photos of our daughters playing in the snow. I often found it was those simple experiences that brought me joy! Our professor emphasized that we practice and take photos of all kinds of subjects no matter what the weather—landscapes, nature, buildings with unique architecture, and people in public places, to name just a few. When we developed them in the dark room, the goal was to achieve strong contrasts and sharpness between the black and gray tones. This course evolved into a metaphor of my life.

After each assignment, there was a day set aside for critiquing. The professor would call on each of us when it was time for us to explain how we did our work. He'd say, "Sandy, you are next, please explain your theme and goals for the assignment." Of course it was nerve wracking but I couldn't wait to show my work. I took pride in what I captured through the lens. I always felt he tried to bring out the best in his students' work by having the critiques. I found it very helpful and learned how to make improvements where needed.

My interest in photography goes back to when I was a child. I loved watching my mother take photos with her Brownie camera and watching my aunt use her movie camera. I followed and listened to them intently. I couldn't wait to see the black and white results after they were printed. "Oh Mother," I said one day, "your prints came today. I can't wait to see them." We eagerly looked at each photo and shared our opinions on whether or not we liked them. There was a significant contrast between seeing still photos and moving pictures. The use of the different cameras had me spellbound.

Since we had no TV in our home, watching silent movies in black and white was fascinating. I am grateful to my aunt for showing them during family events. We saw home movies about travel, nature, and always begged to see the one we called *The Three Bears,* who stole cherry pies from the windowsill at a nearby farm. This was a reel my aunt bought to spice things up, between showing the movies about her trips. We loved her "commercial" reels which were very exciting for us children. As I always said, "Aunt Blanche was a woman ahead of her time!"

One of my favorite black and white photos that I carry with me is of my mother, taken in 1928, when she was 12 years old. When I study the picture, it is as though I'm looking in a mirror. I see myself at that age and wonder what her 12-year-old life was like compared with mine. She was beautiful, with a Mona Lisa smile, a touch of innocence, and a touch of seriousness. When I hold this photo in my hand, I can sense her positive energy.

Even after photography class, I continued to enjoy taking photos on my own and developing them. Nature, landscapes, and people were my focus. The joy of keeping a photo journal helped to hold special memories, and I loved the yin and yang of stark contrasts in the moments I captured in black and white.

I studied some of the famous photographers, such as Ansel Adams (1902-1984) and Dorothea Lange (1895-1965) and was struck by the way they captured the contrasts of black and white along with the many tones of in-between gray. Ansel Adams' work was serene and peaceful. Dorothea Lange's work captured the unemployed men who wandered the streets during the Great Depression, and the families struggling in that horrendous era. She captured the feelings of the people who were her subjects.

Black and white photography reminded me of my life when I was growing up. Sharp rules and regulations were emphasized in our family's religion and my parents' home. Out of those harsh years of learning, the beauty was that I discovered I could develop my life in full color.

# Teaching Art

*"The art of teaching is the art of assisting discovery."*
~Mark Van Doren

Finally, the day arrived! I felt eagerness, anticipation, passion, and joy as I stepped into my new world of teaching. Oh yes, there were a few naysayers warning me I might not get a job right away because of my age and because of the reduced need for teachers. I deliberately ignored those thoughts and listened to my inner voice. I valued those who encouraged me and gained strength from my family and friends who said, "You go girl!" I was on another adventure, and yes, taking another risk—becoming a teacher!

After graduation, I eagerly applied for teaching jobs, and to my surprise, I was called for several interviews. Full of nerves and excitement, I listened to my husband say, "Let them know they need you and you are up for the challenge." I liked that encouragement! I found the interviews to be unique at each school and aimed to answer the questions professionally. "So, why do you want to teach art?" "What kind of experience do you have?" I was always happy to tell them about my journey, experience, and have them view my portfolio. It was important to speak from my heart and be myself. I felt the Divine with me from the very beginning, and I just had to do my part and trust.

The following is a glimpse of my journey—the first two years of teaching kindergarten through twelfth grade. I was helping to fill in for teachers who were on leave of absence. I was thrilled because it gave me great experience and helped me to decide which grade level I enjoyed the most.

First I was asked to teach kindergarten through sixth grade. Teaching at the elementary level, a teacher works very hard trying to keep up with each child's needs, their insecurities, and joys. I soon realized I had to be a mother, a counselor, and a teacher as I listened to all the demands. The children's requests abounded, such as, "Mrs. Miller, I messed up my painting because the paint spilled!" "Mrs. Miller, I feel sick, and I'm going to throw up." "Mrs. Miller, how do you like my work?" In the elementary years, students are like sponges, absorbing everything that is taught. I thrived on the challenges teaching the elementary level and enjoyed every day. To me, this experience was like being a juggler, learning to manage many things at one time.

My second assignment was teaching the middle school level, seventh and eighth grades. This experience was a different world altogether. Seventh graders begin having a mind of their own, and by eighth grade, many appear to be goofy and are somewhat "off the wall" as they try to find themselves and fit in with their peers. Having our own children helped prepare me for this age group and for many reasons I enjoyed the challenge. Most students were cooperative and did their work. If they had issues or had a negative attitude, I would ask them to go out in the hall and have a talk with themselves, tossing in a little attitude surgery on the side before they returned. When they came back into the room, I would ask privately, "So, what did you tell yourself?" One student said, "I told myself I needed to change my behavior and have a better attitude. And myself said 'Okay!'" So, I said, "Great! Now let's get back to work."

I often reminded the students, "Even if you don't like art, we are here to learn and be challenged." My motto was: There is more than one way to draw, paint, and see things. By the end of the year, most students seemed to understand this, and that I would not accept "I can't."

It's funny how some things are carried over from home. When we hosted parent's night at school, I still can hear the parents' voices as they entered my classroom. They'd declare, "I was never good at art," or "I don't have a creative bone in my body," or "I can't even draw a stick person!" I would welcome them in and explain the art curriculum and have them engage in a fun exercise, proving that they were, indeed more creative than they thought they could be.

I had several ideas lined up which they could choose from. Draw ten dots on the paper and then connect the dots. This kind of doodling results in a line drawing, and there are no mistakes—each drawing is unique and perfect "as is." In another exercise, I suggested they take a photo from the stack of portraits on the table, turn it upside down, and draw it from that vantage point. They couldn't believe how well these drawings turned out. Often, when we turn something upside down, we remove the automatic guidance our brains want to provide, and we're able to see more clearly the areas we're attempting to draw. Another exercise was to draw something that they saw in the room. I emphasized for them to really look at the object and follow its lines. "Don't think how it should look," I said, "observe how it does look and draw what you see." The point was to have them do something that showed their ability to succeed. Yes, it helps if you enjoy art, but if you think you're no good at it, that doesn't mean you cannot learn. As a teacher I hung onto my motto: There is more than one way to draw, paint, and see things.

One of the most unexpected experiences I had during my first year was when a seventh grader came into my room after school. He said, "Mrs. Miller, I came to ask you a question. Our youth group at church is trying to earn points to go to church camp, and I wondered if I could massage your feet for fifteen points." I was so taken aback and wondered what was going on. I quickly replied, "No Daryl, it is not appropriate, and I'm asking you to leave now." He slowly left the room with his head hanging. The next day I explained to the principal what happened and he said, "I'm sorry that you were not told about this student who has issues." I said, "Fortunately I handled it with ease, but it sure was strange." Surprises will happen, and the important thing is how you deal with them. I rolled with the punches and stayed calm and in charge when the surprises came along.

Having twenty-five to thirty students in a classroom is a huge challenge for any teacher. I learned quickly and told the students, "I have eyes all over my head so don't try to cause any trouble." Humor, boundaries, and empathy were three things I carried with me in my toolbox. At this age, students needed a different kind of attention than when they were younger. A teacher has to tune in and give encouragement in positive ways and be fair when dealing with problems. Teaching the middle school students was an adventure, and I thrived on the challenges.

Where I taught, all students from kindergarten through the eighth grade were required to take art classes as part of their curriculum. I always felt the exposure to art and learning to see life through that lens made a positive difference in their lives. Students were taught that art is connected to all areas of life: science, math, language arts, history, and social studies. At the beginning of every year, I asked the students to "Look around and tell me what, in this room, is related to art." We discussed color, design, and composition—how the chairs and the tables related to the art of design. Art education included critical thinking and problem solving. Once students comprehended these concepts, it made it easier to teach the various facets of them. I loved teaching them how Leonardo da Vinci was a great example of one who combined art with math and science.

During my second year and third assignment, I was asked to teach at the high school level. I was glad to be one of the older teachers. I felt confident, but I was in new territory. At this age, the students are more independent, and most enjoy being in art class. At that time, art was not a requirement like in kindergarten through eighth grade; it was their choice as an elective course.

I had to learn quickly how to relate to these young adults. I found that getting to know them first, and finding out what their interests were, helped me to connect. Young adults are fascinating to observe and listen to. Some talked about their home life challenges and their dating issues. I remember two girls, best friends, who were in their senior year. On Mondays when they came to class, they always looked sleepy-eyed after the weekend. I sat at their table one day and asked how their weekend was. One of the girls said, "Dating and spending time with boys is exhausting!" I was surprised by her honesty but didn't want to show it, so I changed the subject. With a lot of the conversations I had with students of this age, I realized I was there to listen, be supportive where appropriate, and not make judgments. I was amazed at how expansive senior high students were with their creativity, and they inspired me with their artwork. I looked for the good in every student even though sometimes they were a challenge.

High school students are fortunate when they can choose to sign up for art classes they are interested in, such as drawing, painting, ceramics, photography, and computer arts. This opportunity allows them to pursue many areas they might want to specialize in after high school.

As I reflect on my years of teaching I can honestly say I loved it. Sometimes I made mistakes, but mistakes are a great source of learning. At that point in my career, I decided I enjoyed teaching at the middle school level the most. The following year I was asked to teach in another school district and to my delight, ended up in the middle school where I taught for 13 years.

Students can be great teachers, and I enjoyed learning from them as well. Following my dream wasn't always easy but seeing it come true was a gift to myself.

# Education through Travel

*"The best education I have ever received was through travel."*
-Lisa Ling

I often thought, *I wish students could actually see parts of the world rather than just studying from books. They might appreciate, and remember more if they could see up close the people and places they are learning about.* Thank goodness for field trips. Going on field trips during my youth was exciting and I think those experiences made me want to see the world even more. I realize today with television and social media that images and information about other places are right at our fingertips. And with transportation relatively affordable and widely available, young people have many opportunities to experience travel. I, on the other hand, grew up with limited options, only seeing Bible pictures of different countries and the National Geographic magazine at home. I would daydream and wonder what it would be like to go to places like Africa and the Middle East. My mother would say, "Let's look at the map and see where they are located." She loved geography and that rubbed off on me. To this day I love studying a paper map even though Google maps on my phone will tell me every turn I need to take to arrive at my destination.

While I was growing up our family took very few vacations, because farm life kept us homebound. Vacations were a luxury when I was young. So picnics and going to the local state parks are some of my good memories of exploration outside the boundaries of home. In high school, our junior and senior class went to Washington, D.C. and to New York on bus trips. Those experiences are etched in my mind and inspired me to travel.

219

One day a friend of mine asked, "Sandra, my brother and I plan to take a trip to Phoenix, Arizona to visit my sister and your brother this summer. Would you like to go with us?" I said, "Like to go? Of course I'd *love* to, but I'll have to ask my parents first." I was sixteen so I wasn't sure if I'd be allowed, but to my relief my parents said yes. The trip was a huge adventure and lots of fun. My friend's brother drove and we two girls sat in the back seat, taking in the landscapes and laughing at funny signs—like a sign that said, "Cattle XING" with a picture of people underneath instead of cows. We were amazed at how flat the land was and to see so many adobe homes gave us a glimpse into another culture. It was so exciting to travel this far. I had to pinch myself to make sure this was really happening. We had a wonderful visit with our siblings and had the opportunity to learn more about the Native American culture. It was an educational trip!

There is a song that comes to mind when I think of traveling, called, "I've Been Everywhere," written by Geoff Mack in 1959 and popularized by many famous musicians, including Johnny Cash. Of course, I haven't been everywhere but it sure feels good to have seen many different places. Those who have seen parts of the world that are different from where they grew up are fortunate. Travel is an educational opportunity that often far surpasses book learning about different places and cultures!

After my husband and I got married we were very fortunate to be able to travel. We were adventuresome, and many times we went to various places on a whim. One year, close to Christmas, I said to Carlton, "Why don't we go to London for Christmas this year, for a long weekend?" We both agreed and made plans to go. Little did we know how they celebrated Christmas in London. I had imagined it would be like New York, with lots of lights and excitement and the hustle and bustle of shopping. To our surprise, we found that it was quite the opposite of what we'd expected, and everything seemed quiet while most people stayed inside.

Through the years, Carlton and I traveled to all the U.S. states except Hawaii. We visited London, Germany, Switzerland, Austria, Lichtenstein, China, Ireland, Argentina, Brazil, Peru, Bolivia, Paraguay, Uruguay, and Canada. What I remember most were the kind hearted people, hardworking people, different religions, different music, delicious food, and appreciating all the differences. I realize now how we all have things in common with other people around the world. We might have our differences, but we're all connected. Through traveling I feel I have taken many courses in history, religion, and social studies. I've learned more about people and diverse cultures than I would have from just reading books.

Traveling continues to be an education for Carlton and me. We never stop learning, and the more we talk with people who are different, the less fear we have of those differences. Education comes in many packages and traveling is one of the great ones.

## PART FOUR

# Mountain Adventures

# Moving to the Mountains

*"When I wake up every morning, I smile and say, 'Thank you.' Because out of my window I can see the mountains, then go hiking with my dog and share her bounding joy in the world."* ~Carole King

Carlton asked me one wintry evening while we were sitting beside a roaring fire in the hearth, "If we both want to move again, where would it be?" It was an interesting question because we had just moved five years prior, to this cozy house in the country, not far from the small town of Akron, PA where we had lived for twenty-five years, and raised our daughters. We both had good jobs, and we were happy, but something was urging us to pursue another adventure. I thought for a moment of all the places we had enjoyed visiting. I said, "You know we love New Mexico, Arizona, and Colorado. But I don't know if we want to move that far from Pennsylvania." He agreed and said, "What about another place in the mountains of Pennsylvania?"

We loved our current home because it was located in the country, in a wooded area with whitetail deer meandering through our yard. And it was a place where I could finally have a flower garden. I planted almost a hundred day lilies of all colors. I was in heaven watching the flowers bloom. The variety of birds made me want to sing along with them. It was a place where we felt close to nature and sensed that we were connected to all of it.

As we sat by the fire, we had fun talking about where to move. I said, "We certainly loved where we lived during the first two years of our marriage. State College, Pennsylvania, was a great place and we could see mountains in every direction." I often mentioned after coming down Seven Mountains, while traveling towards State College, "This truly feels like Happy Valley," (which is a well-known nickname for the territory of State College). "Those mountains are awesome and they make me happy!"

Carlton agreed and said, "For fun, should we check to see if there is land for sale near State College?" I got excited and said, "Yes, let's do our research and explore." We started reading more about State College and the surrounding towns. For fun, I checked to see how many bed and breakfast places were in the area. After deciding to take on this adventure, I retired from teaching the following year, and Carlton continued to work until it was time to move.

We called a realtor in State College and met with her the next week. "Hello Millers," she said, "my name is Barbara and I'm ready to show you around." I knew we were off to a good start because her name was the same as my mother's. The realtor was a nice lady who was eager to help us. Plus, she really tuned in to what we were looking for. That was a gift! We told Barbara we wanted at least 20 acres of land, no more than 20 miles from Penn State and it had to have a good view. Every time she found a place for sale, she called, and we went that weekend to see the places she had to show us.

Month after month we looked at many charming places in the mountains. One time I said, "It's one thing to be in the mountains, but another thing to be too isolated and far from stores." Yes, we were very particular about where we wanted to perch. Different times I would think, *Would I like to be stuck out here all by myself?* We kept looking and one bright day, after about ten months of looking, Barbara showed us land on the Allegheny Front near Black Moshannon State Park. The land was 56 acres of woodland on the south side of the mountain, with a 5-acre meadow near the access road. We walked the area and then sat together on a large flat rock that was part way up the hillside on the property. We looked out at the view over the meadow and treetops and we both agreed it was a little piece of heaven. We told Barbara we were interested but had to think about it. I prayed, *May the Divine help us to make the right decision.*

Once again we set out on the now familiar trip from State College, back to Lancaster. You know how it is when you are riding in a car for a few hours. Sometimes you talk nonstop and others times you're quiet and reflective. On that trip home from the little piece of heaven, we experienced both. We discussed our thoughts and ideas and then began to daydream quietly. I said, "I liked how the land was some distance from the main road. I also noticed neighbors nearby, hidden by all the trees." Carlton said, "I agree and it is a great place to observe nature." I started daydreaming again, *I could have a big flower garden and make stone walls along the lane.* There were rocks everywhere, and then I thought, *But that means snakes! Ok, I might have to face my fears again.*

After making several visits and hiking around the 56 acres, we were getting more excited each time. I said, "Let's go to the big rock again, to sit and think about it." We had so much fun observing nature with our eagle eyes. Carlton said, "Wouldn't this be a great place to build a log house, right below this rock, and make it a bed and breakfast so we could share it with others?" I said, "This is an awesome place to build, and that's a great idea!" We soon announced to Barbara that we wanted to buy the land and start dreaming about building. She said, "I think this is a great spot and the view really adds to its beauty." We were over the moon with excitement!

Elation is another word that defined the moment and now it was time to find a reliable builder to build our log house/bed and breakfast. Barbara gave us a list of builders whom we called and interviewed. After doing our research, we discovered this would not be a simple dwelling to build. Again, we felt the Divine working with us as we found DeHaas Builders in State College. Talk about wonderful people coming into our lives! We met the father and son who worked together with a great team of qualified people.

Now that we had found a high-quality builder, Carlton said, "Someone has to check on the project as the house is being built. Since I'm still working full-time, would you mind being the manager of our project? Since I had retired from my teaching job I said, "Sure, I think that would be fun." It took nine months to build and almost every week I drove two hours up to State College to check on our future home and business. It was a fun experience watching how the builders worked. What an education! I was amazed with the crew's skills and how well they worked together. Week after week I kept a record of the progress and the questions and concerns that arose.

On weekends while our house was being built, we stayed at a bed and breakfast in State College. We loved being on the mountain as much as possible to observe nature, and check the progress of the building project. I had lots of fun planning ideas for flowerbeds and building stone walls beside the long lane. I find it difficult to put into words how awesome this experience was. Nature has a way of bringing joy and time for reflection.

In nine months our log house was built, including plenty of space for our bed and breakfast amenities on the first floor. We asked several friends, "Any ideas for a good name for our bed and breakfast?" Our friends Skip and Chris were always witty and I can still hear Skip saying, "What about calling it The Snaky Hill B&B?" He knew full well that snakes were not my friends and he was teasing me. I said, "Yeah right, and that will draw people to our bed and breakfast bigtime." I said, "I'm sure you can come up with something more appropriate." He said, "Well, this place is hidden here in the mountains, what about Mountain Hideaway Bed and Breakfast?" Carlton and I said, "Yes, that one is perfect with or without the snakes in our midst!"

For sixteen years we enjoyed our Mountain Hideaway. Carlton worked a full-time job in State College and I managed the bed and breakfast. By choice I did not hire any help. Going from teaching to being a hostess was tons of fun—hard work, yes, but I loved the routine, meeting interesting people, and the nurturing that my new position allowed me to indulge in for our guests. Every job has its downside, but I learned early in life how important it is to have a positive mindset about doing work whether we enjoy it or not. Seriously, who really loves to clean?

Moving to this mountain was one of our highlights in life. I loved working on the land as well as managing the bed and breakfast. Carlton said one day, "I can't believe you cleared the whole meadow!" I said, "Yes, this place really brought the farm girl out in me. I loved every minute of clearing the briars and brush with the weed whacker and mower." It all paid off because after it was cleared, we could see the wild turkeys, bears with their young cubs, deer, and bobcats walking through the meadow. I said one day while watching a mother bear nursing her cub right in the middle of the meadow, "I think the animals know the meadow is a safe place to be!"

Each year the flowers and plants flourished. People came from many interesting places. Many found Mountain Hideaway online or through word of mouth. We were happy when they returned each year. We had visitors from many faraway regions, such as Germany, France, England, Africa, Australia, India, Russia, Dubai, and Canada. And Penn State alumni were always fun people to have as guests since we are Penn State fans, and Carlton an alumnus.

# Treasure Beyond Broken Glass

*"Moments, rather than possessions, are the true treasures of life."*
-Frank Sonnenberg

It was a beautiful rainy day, a chance for me to work inside to clean and organize. It was the year 2000 and we had just moved to our log house in the mountains, near State College, Pennsylvania, a majestic place to live on the Allegheny Front where the deer roamed freely, the bear passed through the meadow, and wild turkeys often visited. We were on another special adventure. This land was a piece of heaven to live on and start our bed and breakfast enterprise.

With excitement, I found myself carefully choosing the dishes and glassware my mother gave me, deciding what to display in my china cupboard. My mother had died five years prior to this move and now I was standing there alone in my thoughts as I chose and felt each piece, feeling Mother's loving presence. I missed her more than I can put into words.

She loved her fine tea sets, ruby red sherbet bowls, and her crystal water glasses. Putting them into the china cupboard brought back so many memories of when she had used them for company. I got all choked up when I realized she wouldn't be able to help me unpack, and this was a place she would never see with her physical eyes.

What I loved was how she had divided her things between us seven children as she grew into her elder years. One day my mother invited us to get together at her place. She lined up seven empty boxes with our names attached and asked my sister-in-law to help her put some special things in each one. She would hold up a tea set, for example, and ask one of us "Whose am I touching?" and when it was our turn, we could claim it for ourselves or name another sibling. It was so much fun, and very meaningful, but sad at the same time. It was her way of downsizing, letting go, and sharing the stories that went with the items and the meaning they had for her. She would say, "This fruit bowl is from your Aunt Catherine," or "My mother gave me this blue fruit bowl when I got married." I was so happy I got the butter mold, her set of glasses, and the beautiful ruby red goblets that she used to serve her homemade fruit salad. She loved geography, so it was no surprise that she was proud to say where the dishes came from. She would cheerfully announce, "Look at this blue floral bowl! It came all the way from Germany!" and another time, "This plate is from France!" My mother appreciated everything she had, and these things I inherited were treasures to me as well.

Memories swirled in my mind, reminding me of how often Mother had entertained company and how she had enjoyed setting her table fit for a queen. I loved when she used her fine glass goblets, small glass salt dishes with tiny glass serving spoons, and her very best china. We were common people, farmers to be exact, so our everyday world was simple, but Mother loved to use the best whenever people came to visit.

As I was putting things away, I wondered if she had ever wished to live in a nicer house and have finer things. She never revealed her feelings or complained about what she didn't have, but always made things look and feel special no matter what kind of house she lived in or who came to visit.

As I was arranging the shiny dishes and elegant ruby red depression glasses Mother gave me, I walked over to the table to pick up more glasses to put into the cupboard. All of a sudden there was a loud crash. I turned around and to my shock two shelves had fallen on top of each other, breaking Mother's glassware into smithereens. I stood there, numb. There was nothing I could do! Many of the glasses were shattered into hundreds of pieces. I felt sick to my stomach and overwhelmingly sad.

That is when I heard my mother's voice say, "These are only things. Hold dear the good memories." I was also reminded of the Bible verse she often quoted when I was growing up, "Lay not up for yourselves treasures upon earth, where moth and rust doth corrupt, and where thieves break through and steal. But lay up for yourselves treasures in heaven, where neither moth nor rest doth corrupt, and where thieves do not break through nor steal. For where your treasure is, there will your heart be also."[2] My mother "walked her talk" and was a great example to her seven children. Though she lived simply and didn't have many fancy or fine things, she valued sharing those things she did have, and was joyful and content.

As I reflected on the broken shards of glass, I was reminded of life and how fragile it can be. Things have value, glass is beautiful, but things and glass are only as powerful as the love and joy behind them. This broken glass was a reminder to me that unexpected events happen in life. And the question always remains: How will I handle those unexpected, painful situations? In this case, I remembered the importance of treasuring the memories of Mother and keeping the faith. The broken glass itself brought temporary sadness, but the beautiful lessons from my mother will be with me forever, and that is treasure indeed.

---

[2] Matthew 6:19-21

# Mountain Hideaway
# Bed and Breakfast

*"All experience is education for the soul." ~ Unknown*

Carlton and I love adventure and taking on new challenges. After all, we married each other. We've been married over fifty years and what a trip we've been on.

During the beginning stages of running our bed and breakfast business, we were very concerned about doing everything right. One learns quickly what works and what doesn't. In a short time, we had things down to a science when it came to the work. No need to sweat the small stuff.

One morning I was up early, easing into my rituals, sipping coffee, reading and doing e-mail, as usual. I love mornings! No way do you want to run a bed and breakfast if you are not a morning person! On this particular morning, I remember feeling fantastic as I was watching the sunrise and being thankful for the fun-filled guests who had made reservations.

I prepared my menu and had everything ready on time for the 9:00 o'clock breakfast. As usual, I turned the oven on low, fifteen minutes before serving the food. Our guests were sitting around the table talking and laughing, always a delight to hear. I began serving the juice and fruit and then returned to my kitchen to take the "To Die for French Toast" and "Baked Egg Dish" out of the oven when I discovered I could not open the oven door. I thought that was strange because I had never had a problem before.

To my horror, I now noticed I had not turned the oven on low. I had turned on the cleaning button! I went flying downstairs to check the circuit box to turn off the switch. I came flying back up, and to my disappointment, I still could not open the door. An oven has a mind of its own. And has to run the whole cycle for cleaning! No interruptions! I would not be able to use it until hours later. The food was done for!

Eight people were at the table ready to eat one of my favorite menus, and I am now looking through the glass oven window, watching the French toast burn to a crisp along with the blessed baked egg dish. I knew I couldn't serve ashes, so I had to think quickly of something creative. Keep in mind these guests saw me running to and fro but didn't know how to interpret my behavior.

I pulled myself together and announced serenely how happy I was that they were having a wonderful time. As the guests enjoyed their coffee and orange juice, I hesitantly confessed to what I had done. I told them if they gave me fifteen more minutes I was sure I could whip up something wonderful for them to eat. After all, guests pay for bed and breakfast, not just for the bed!

Within fifteen minutes, I whipped up yet another French toast recipe, called "Plain Old French Toast," which I cooked on the stovetop. To my delight, the guests were as happy as larks with my presentation. They said it was the best French toast they had ever eaten. Bless them. Bless my wonderful stovetop.

We never know how we will respond in a crisis, but one thing I do know for sure is that life happens. As I often said, "It is not what happens to us that matters most; it is how we deal with it!" Those guests continued to return. We still laugh remembering how that morning, breakfast turned into a circus. After all the acrobatics, breakfast was served and eaten with smiles all 'round.

French toast anyone?

# It's All About the Guests!

*"We see our customers as invited guests to a party, and we are the hosts. It's our job every day to make every important aspect of the customer experience a little bit better."*
-Jeff Bezos

"So, how do you enjoy running a bed and breakfast?" the guests would ask. I said, "Truthfully, I love the work. I did not go into the job glamorizing what it might be like."

I said I made choices after we decided to follow through with the idea. It was my nature to have a checklist of things to do, whenever I started a new project. I researched how many other bed and breakfasts were in the area. I found out what advertising was required and read about the B&B Association and became a member. I made a list of what items were needed for the guest rooms and for the common area. This was a new experience but I felt confident and began having fun planning the details. Some guests shared how they would dream of having a bed and breakfast, kind of romanticizing the idea. I was happy to share my experiences with guests who were considering becoming B&B owners.

I said, "It helps to be a morning person, willing to work hard and enjoy being with people, stay flexible and always remember guests come first!" We only had three guest rooms so I decided not to hire help. I was always used to working hard so it made sense to try it myself. I planned my days around having guests, gardening, lawn work, and cleaning more than I liked. I often said, "Every job has its downside and cleaning was probably the downer for me in this job." I enjoyed everything else and I loved the fact I had a variety of things to work on, including arts and crafts, after I got the B&B work routine in place. I joined the Women's Welcome Club of State College and got involved with activities they offered. I loved it all!

Per the online dictionary by Merriam-Webster, one definition for guest is "a person to whom hospitality is extended." I strongly believe that if you don't enjoy being around people with all kinds of needs this job would not be for you. When guests stepped inside the door I would note their mannerisms, observe the way they talked to me and to each other. "Please" and "thank you" certainly go a long way, but a few guests were demanding, and those words were not spoken by them. It didn't take me long to learn that some people are not into socializing and prefer to be left alone. Some loved to talk and engage in conversation. I tried to respond in kind.

I only had a handful of guests who really tested my patience in those sixteen years. In those cases, I asked myself, "What can I learn from those who are more of a challenge?" There were many teachable moments and I learned the most from figuring out how to deal with the issues that came along. I'd think to myself, *Do I have some of the same flaws this person has?* Usually there was more to their story than I knew. Isn't that true in many situations? We don't always know the whole story! If I believed "guests came first" then I had to be prepared for all kinds of personalities and think of their comfort before my own.

What I learned over and over again is that we all have similar needs, and oftentimes similar flaws. It is up to us to show love and compassion to others. Many guests shared their stories, such as healing from an illness, or dealing with a life-threatening disease. Some had recently lost a loved one or were going through the empty nest transition after their children left home. Others had more joyful experiences, such as seeing their child graduate from college, having a family reunion, or attending a wedding. We also had mother and daughter gatherings, as well as families meeting at Mountain Hideaway who traveled from different locations, such as Ohio and New York, finding a central location at our B&B.

Running a bed and breakfast was fun for me. It helped me to be broadminded and open to learning and finding out what the guests liked. I had guests ask all the usual questions, like "How late do you allow people to check in?" "Do you allow children?" "Do you allow pets?" Thankfully all the answers were stated on our website and in our brochures so I could provide information easily to avoid confusion and smooth out their arrival experience. I still tried to be polite in answering; going out of my way and trying to make people feel at home. Unfortunately, I could not please everyone. For example, one guest knew we didn't take pets but they brought a pet anyway and left their pet in their car. I only found out after the fact. Probably not the best experience for their pet, but at least they didn't bring it into the house as far as we knew, as we weren't prepared for ongoing animal residency and the cleaning and preparation that involves.

For sixteen years I taught in the public schools and for sixteen years I ran a bed and breakfast. Through these positions I learned a lot about myself, and in that learning I realized that regardless of the position, the important lessons in life all come down to how we treat others. I am no saint; I don't have tons of patience, and sometimes I talk too much, but I do recognize what it means to be unfair, unkind, and self-centered. Practice makes better in every area! I am convinced we need to take care of ourselves first in order to be worthwhile to others. I feel very blessed having the job opportunities that I took on because they have helped me to grow. Guests come first because when we put ourselves into the position of caretaker, it really is all about them!

# Bears

*"The best way of being kind to bears is not to be very close to them."* -Margaret Atwood

Every morning Carlton and I would wake up to beautiful sunrises, and sometimes watched heavy clouds dance over the mountain ridges. It always left us awe-inspired. Each day the mountains hugged us as a reminder not to take them for granted. We never got tired of seeing God's beauty and inspiration. The change of seasons always brought new insights about nature. I said to him, "Living here on the mountain always reminds me of a verse I memorized when I was young." "I will lift up mine eyes unto the hills, from whence cometh my help. My help cometh from the LORD, which made heaven and earth." Psalm 121:1 & 2, King James Version. I continue to recite this verse almost daily.

Carlton and I were always anxious for springtime to arrive, because that was the season to see the bears come down the mountain. They were very special guests indeed! The mother with her cubs and sometimes the huge 500 lb males appeared. During the sixteen years we lived there I learned that if we showed respect to the bears, they in return respected us. In other words we knew not to get in their way and never to get between a mother and her cubs.

The first year we lived there, I said to Carlton, "I would love to start feeding the birds but it's important where we put the feeders because of the bears." He said, "Let's try putting the feeders up high on a line and see if it works." So we did, until one morning we saw that a feeder had been knocked down and we noticed bear tracks underneath where it had been. I said, "Well, I can see the picnic table in the meadow from our great room, why don't we put the feed there on the table?" What a sight to behold! The variety of birds was awesome to see but to our disappointment, short-lived.

Soon after we put the food on the table for the birds, there she sat, the mother bear on the bench like a human being, with her three cubs walking around on the picnic table. This reminded me of the *Winnie the Pooh* stories. The scene took my breath away because we got to see the bears closer than we ever had before. I said, hoping that somehow the bears would hear me, "Remember, the feed we put on the table is for the birds!" We knew not to feed the bears, but for a short time we kept putting feed on the table for the birds! And of course the bears kept coming. I said, "I think they are beginning to invite some of their friends to join them because I see more than the mother and her three cubs."

I kept justifying feeding the birds because how else does one get a chance to study them this close? What I learned about bears is that the mothers do an outstanding job of protecting their cubs. It was a pure delight to watch. For example, one day the mother and her three cubs were walking through the meadow and they came to the water trough. The cubs were playing and having a grand time. All of a sudden I heard some loud sounds. I looked down in the meadow and saw a huge male bear coming toward the mother bear. I read that males sometimes try to kill the cubs. I watched intently and was amazed. The mother made a sound for the cubs to go up a nearby tree. They were quick and obedient! The male was a huge threat and for about 45 minutes the mother bear stood her ground until the male bear finally gave up and moseyed away. Talk about courage and not giving up! When the male left, the little ones slowly came down from the tree one by one and followed their mother into the forest. According to what I read, males often kill the cubs in order to mate with the mother bear. Nature is full of mystery and I had trouble understanding this! It became clear when I found out that female bears will not mate as long as they're still nursing and raising their cubs, which can be many months to two years, according to wildlife biologist, Sean Farley.

I said to Carlton, "I think the bear and I have an understanding of motherhood. Any time she sees me outside working, she looks in my direction and seems to smile, knowing I'm not a threat to her and her cubs." I would often walk outside when they were in the meadow and when she saw me she kept on enjoying her duties. Each year we would see the same mother, and later new mothers, with their cubs. Their behavior was very similar. They watched over their cubs intently.

One time we saw the mother bear nursing her cubs in the meadow, right out in the open! This was a rare sight to observe. Another time we noticed the cubs were high up in the tree and the mother walked over and went into the wooded area. I said, "I wonder how she gets her little ones to come down?" The most beautiful scene was to see her come out of the woods and go over to the tree, hugging it as she looked up to send a signal with a noise and scent for them to come down. Slowly, one by one they came down after their nap to regroup. One cub took forever to come down, but she patiently waited and then they all walked up the mountain, homeward bound.

Elena Harris, of http://www.spiritanimalinfo writes that the primary meaning of the bear spirit is "strength and confidence," and I would agree, after observing how they live and take care of themselves. Sometimes I encountered bears closer than I wanted them to be while working outside. But I always found that if I used common sense and backed away they would go on their way. Oh for the love of bears!

# Deer in the Meadow

*"I ask people why they have deer heads on their walls. They always say because it's such a beautiful animal. There you go. I think my mother is attractive, but I have photographs of her."* ~Ellen DeGeneres

Ever since I was a child I loved nature, whether it was sitting under the weeping willow tree watching birds at the farm, or observing ants on the ground working on their chores. Nature has always made me curious and has also brought me peace.

I said to Carlton, "We were blessed to live at Mountain Hideaway for sixteen years, a place where nature surrounded us each day." He agreed, because he loved watching nature as much as I did. In fact he stopped hunting after we moved away from our parents' homes and said he had lost interest. He said, "I only went hunting to be with my father, but deep down, I never really enjoyed the hunting part of it." One of the precious events each year at Mountain Hideaway was to watch the deer and fawns in our meadow below the house. To observe the mothers care for their fawns brought a lot of joy.

By early May, we would begin to see baby fawns and this would continue through June. Amazingly the mother would often hide them right after they were born. I loved the colors of their white spots against the bronze of their fur that glowed in the sunlight and was great camouflage in dappled sunshine. It is a majestic sight to watch the fawns nurse and learn to walk. I said to Carlton, "Look how the mother protects them by hiding them close to our house, away from predators like the hawks and black bears in the open meadow." Carlton always said, "They know what they are doing!"

One day while I was mowing the high grass in the meadow I saw a newborn fawn all curled up in a ball in the grass. I was so thankful I saw her in time because I would have been devastated if I hurt her! I watched in awe as the little darling slowly got up on her wobbly legs and tried to walk. She hobbled into the woods where her mother came to meet her. I called her Bambi.

I always felt these connections with nature were sacred and the deer showed a spirit of gentleness, love, and care. The mother would nurse for about two weeks and then gradually the fawns learned to eat grass. Within six weeks, the little ones were able to function completely independently but stayed with their mother until the next set of fawns. We often saw the little ones frolicking in the meadow, chasing each other like children on a playground. I think through watching nature I experienced lessons that reminded me how love and care goes a long way with humans, as much as it does in the wild.

I truly love the deer and fawns and marvel at how they live and survive. Yes, they are free, but always on the lookout for predators, and if the mothers have fawns, they work extra hard to protect them. Usually we would see a mother with one or two fawns in the meadow, but rarely three. I thought, *Just like the bear, the deer come to the meadow as though they know it is a safe haven.*

*"Animals, like us, are living souls. They are not things.*
*They are not objects. Neither are they human. Yet they*
*mourn. They love. They dance. They suffer. They know the*
*peaks and chasms of being."* ~Gary Kowalski

### Bobcat's Bad Hair Day
### Sandra L. Miller

Seeing nature outside my window is a pure delight,
Birds, chipmunks, wild turkeys, and bobcats by night.

Like most cats, bobcats look with sharp eyes on a mission,
Looking left then right, stalking a rabbit for nutrition.

I never tire of watching their gestures, like a bobbing head as they stride by,
Looking eagerly, sometimes stopping to rest, and then trotting off to hide.

I'd like to see a litter of babies, born between April and May,
But they are out of sight, protected by their mother's care every day.

I read that bobcats can jump as high as 12 feet and run 34 miles per hour,
I'm sure I would not want to be in their way with all that power.

The memories are precious as I watch bobcats come and go,
I have to chuckle sometimes when they move rather slow.

I imagine when they meander through our meadow, looking rather glum,
*Another bad hair day, more hunting to do, but it has to be done.*

# The Frog's Dilemma

*"Know that the same spark of life that is within you, is within all of our animal friends, the desire to live is the same within all of us..."* ~Rai Aren

One lovely morning as I was leaving the garage to go outside and work, I heard a strange, rather robust noise. It sounded like it was coming from the pond so I slowly went to check it out. There she was, a screaming frog dangling between two rocks.

I said out loud, "Oh dear, it looks you are stuck between the rocks, I'll be right over to help you!" I ran over and lifted up the rock and to my horror a snake was to blame, holding tightly onto the frog's leg. Of course, I yelled, and if you know me, you know that I have a primal fear of snakes. My husband, the snake charmer, taught me how to detect a poisonous snake from the non-poisonous kind. He explained, "Just look at the shape of their eyeballs. If the pupils are slits, it is most likely venomous, and if the pupils are round, they are most likely non-venomous." *Yeah right,* I thought to myself, *I'm going to get closer and check!* For me, they all look the same, which of course is my excuse for not wanting to get closer than I have to. Yes, intellectually I get it when they say, "Face your fears." Well I do, but in a different way.

The funny thing is, I really enjoy watching frogs even though I know full well there are also poisonous frogs on the planet. In this situation, I wasn't sure how to help the frog because I didn't want to deal with the snake. Carlton informed me that the snake was not poisonous or the frog would already be dead. I said, "No frog should have to experience a slow death like this, and I had to do something!"

I decided to go get a long pole and press it against the snake's head to free the frog. It worked and the frog went wobbling all over the place in the pond, trying to recover, first on his back and then on his belly. I felt like I had to be the referee so I yelled, "Go, go and get out of sight to the lower pond!" It was a sight to behold. The frog got away and went over the falls to the pond below. The snake was mad as a hornet because I messed up his meal. He slowly slithered around the rocks which lined the pond. I hoped the frog went to a safe place because I could tell the snake was not going to give up. Soon he was out of sight.

The next morning, I got up early and as usual looked outside over the pond and meadow. Hilarious! There she was, the frog in the top pond looking up at me. I laughed out loud because she looked like she was smiling to let me know she was fine. And then she winked. My guess is that all her frog friends were watching as I tried to save her because I heard a lot of joyful croaking that morning.

Frogs are frogs and snakes are snakes. I will need attitude surgery to deal with snakes. I understand how nature works but I always had a difficult time with the theory of the survival of the fittest. It is what it is and I have to accept the ways of Mother Nature, although given the chance, I take pride in saving a frog from a snake.

# Lessons from Wild Geese

*"If we all have as much sense as geese, we will stand by
each other in difficult times as well as when we are strong."*
~Dr. Robert McNeish

There is no doubt that we lived in the perfect setting to observe nature.
We had the wooded area surrounding us, and the lush meadow out front.
A few miles away there was Black Moshannon State Park with its large
man-made lake. This was truly a gift, as it drew the wild geese, and we
thoroughly enjoyed watching them come and go.

In the fall, the wild geese would fly from the lake at Black Moshannon,
over our house, and around in a large circle. I said to Carlton, "Well, this
morning they made their practice run again. It was another beautiful sight."
I was always in awe, watching them as they flew in their V formation. I
would softly thank them for flying over again; it felt as though they knew
I'd be there watching. It was always bittersweet to see them leave in the fall.
It seemed they waited as long as possible to take off for good. It depended
on how long the warm weather lasted. So their departure each fall was a
sure sign that winter was approaching.

I was curious about how the leader trades positions with others during
flight. I found out that the reason the leader falls back in line is that the
leadership position is the hardest, with the most wind resistance, requiring
more energy to beat their wings. When they are tired and fall back, they fly
slightly behind and below another goose, which helps them to save some
energy. I saw this exchange of the leadership position many times during
their practice runs. What an amazing demonstration of teamwork.

The geese follow the same migratory path every year, with familiar stops along the way to refuel, much the same way we plan our travels to visit distant places. Most geese will travel this same pathway all their lives. They like to eat vegetation growing at the bottom of lakes, and some will eat fish as well as insects. After rest and food, they take off again as a group, to continue on their journey of migration to the warmer climes of the North American continent.

One time I was talking with our guests about geese, as I always liked to share a little trivia. I asked them, "Do you know how far a flock of geese can fly in one day?" "No," they said, "how far?" "1500 miles!" I declared. It always amazed me that they could fly that far in a day. I learned that it's because of teamwork that they can do that. The V formation that they create reduces wind resistance so they can spend more time gliding and less energy beating their wings.

I thought it was pretty special to find out that wild geese mate for life and each year the females return to the same nesting sight to lay their eggs. Like many other birds and animals, the bonds of goose families are very strong. Both parents pay attention to the nest while the eggs are incubating, and the goslings are able to communicate with their parents through tapping their egg shells even before they're born. After the goslings hatch, they stay close with their family for up to a year. From their parents they learn all of the important things, such as how to communicate, what to eat, how to swim, and how to fly. When they are older they will follow their parents' migration path year after year.

Carlton and I always looked forward to springtime when the geese returned. If I was fortunate enough to be at home, I would hear them and get a warm feeling inside. I'd run out on the deck to wave and welcome them, and like every year, they would circle over our house as though to say, "We're back!" and then continue their flight to the lake at Black Moshannon.

Some people have told me, "Geese are dirty!" They've said, "If you live where I do, you would get sick of them because they create a lot of filth." Of course I would not argue with them, but I love the wild geese nonetheless. They have a place on this beautiful earth and of course have been here for a very long time. They can teach us many good lessons about family and how to stick together through thick and thin. They show us the value of teamwork and are creatures that are certainly devoted to their mate and young ones. In fact, if a goose drops out of formation during flight, and doesn't have the energy to stay with the group, two other geese will follow that goose to the ground to rest and heal if possible. If the goose ends up dying, the two geese will stay until the end, and only after death has occurred, will they fly to catch up to their original group, or join another formation. Their migration patterns are amazing and to think how they care and look out for each other is heartwarming.

We humans can learn many life lessons from the geese.

## PART FIVE

# Appreciating Life

# Chico Our Joy

*"A dog will teach you unconditional love. If you can have
that in your life, things won't be too bad."*
-Robert Wagner


As Carlton and I were anticipating our move from the mountain to the
suburbs, he said, "We really need another dog." Nacho, our twelve-year-old
black lab had died the previous year and we missed him. Carlton said, "It
is your turn to get a lap dog, the kind you've wanted for a very long time."
I was so happy to hear those words because I felt Nacho was like having a
miniature horse in the house. I said, "Nacho was a lovely dog but wasn't
the cuddly kind." While growing up, I was not allowed to have dogs or cats
in the house so having a large dog was an adjustment. Whereas, Carlton
grew up with German shepherds and beagles roaming around in his house.
Nacho was a fine dog and he was wonderful to have with us. We often
went on long walks together and while living in the mountains he served
us well as a great watchdog.

We decided to start looking online for places that had small dogs
available and then we went exploring. What an education of yet another
kind! There are all kinds of dog breeders. To our dismay, we visited one
place that was a puppy mill. It was so sad to see and hear the dogs looking
stressed and not getting the loving attention they needed. We knew we had
to keep looking although we felt sad hearing their cries as we got in the
car and drove away. Animals need love and care as much as children do!

We continued to look online and found a place that looked
interesting—a lady who raised only small dogs. As we looked at the photos

the lady posted, we could tell there was something different about this place. The dogs looked like they were smiling! It appeared these dogs were well taken care of. We decided to visit the farm, which was about 100 miles from our home. When we drove into the lane leading into her beautiful farm we noticed that everything looked clean and organized. That German/Swiss influence was obvious. These people took pride in their farm and kennel.

We met the lady in her office and she said, "I'll bring in the family of three pups for you to see." She raised shih poo dogs and we learned quickly that they are like live teddy bears. Because of the mixed breed they are smart but they also have a stubborn streak in them as well. They are half miniature poodle and half shih tzu. They don't shed, which makes it great for people who are allergic to fur, plus they are not a lot of work. The three darlings marched into the office where we were seated. We still giggle remembering that day.

Two of the pups went right under the chair but the one we saw online came toward us, as though thinking, *Well, here I am, what do you think?* Carlton got down on the floor and started playing with him. This pup reminded us of a small bear cub, fluffy and loveable. We both fell in love with him but decided to wait and think it through. On our way home Carlton said, "Wasn't it interesting how he came to us and the others walked in the other direction?" I said, "Yes, I think that was a sign that he wanted us."

A week later we called the lady to see if the pup was still available and the lady cheerfully said, "Yes, he is still here waiting." We decided this was the right time even though we knew this was a huge step to purchase another dog, because it is very much like raising a child. They take time to train and care for. We told the lady we were interested in the little one who came to us. She said, "I think you will be happy with him." We returned and picked up our little teddy bear.

On our way home, we continued to discuss what to name our pup. We loved the name Nacho for our other dog and out of the clear blue sky, Carlton asked, "What do you think of the name *Chico,* which means little boy, in Spanish?" I said, "Perfect, let's name him Chico." During the two-hour drive home he slept on my lap and every time he woke up we called him by his name. We agreed, the quicker he knows his name, the more comfortable he will feel. These shih poo dogs experience anxiety and get stressed easily so we wanted to do our part to soothe him. Actually, he did really well riding in the car but was happy when we got home.

We had everything prepared for Chico when we got home. A small gated area with food and water and a crate to help train him, which, to him, should have felt like a safe little nest. Little did we know that he would never adjust to the crate because the lady allowed the dogs to roam in wide open spaces. It took us a year to train Chico because he had his mind made up as to how he wanted help. Night after night he would bark in his crate and we were beginning to wonder whether it was good for him. We decided to call our reliable trainer and went to see if he could help us. He observed the three of us and at the end said, "There is no doubt in my mind that Chico is the king of the mountain! Shih poo dogs have a need to be with people almost 24/7." He gave us some suggestions and even suggested that we try keeping him in the garage in the crate where we couldn't hear him. That suggestion didn't go over very well.

When we got home Carlton said, "I know you said you would never have a dog in our bed, but maybe we should try it, or at least put his bed nearby in our room." With age sometimes we melt, and see things with new eyes. As much as I didn't want to give in, because I'm a light sleeper to begin with, I said, "Okay, let's try it and see if it works." Low and behold Chico became a nearly perfect dog ever after that night. He was easier to work with for training and he seemed much more relaxed. We were amazed. That experience changed us both and I realized it helped for me to have an open mind.

We have had several dogs over the years, but none like Chico. He is so loving and affectionate. Wherever we are in the house, that's where he wants to be. He is constantly attuned by listening, and checking on us. He often falls asleep on top of one of the chairs, but sometimes I think he just pretends because in a blink, he is wide eyed and checking to see where we are. If we are near Chico, he lets us know if he wants to continue to nap or have us play with him. Sometimes we need that special interlude as much he does.

Chico has found a place in our hearts that only a special dog could fill. He is now seven years old and he brings us joy every day!

# Turning Seventy

*"Every year should teach you something valuable; whether
you get the lesson is up to you. Every year brings you closer
to expressing your whole and healed self."* ~Oprah Winfrey

When I was young, I thought life moved slowly and I had plenty of time
to do everything I wanted. But turning seventy was a jolt to my system. I
thought, *My life is moving faster than a jet plane!* I thought to myself, *How,
did this happen? It felt like I just turned fifty, and that was twenty years ago.*
It was like seventy snuck up on me and took me by surprise. But then I
stopped and realized I had been doing what I wanted to do for a good
number of those years. Carlton and I both had good jobs and we enjoyed
our work as well as our home life. I wondered, *Is that what made the time
fly so quickly?*

I loved having birthday parties for others and sometimes for myself.
This time I decided to celebrate and throw myself a party with the help of
my family. I invited about seventy people. It was such a joy to see everyone
who came to help celebrate my birthday. These were my family members,
siblings, and friends, some of whom had been part of my life for fifty years
or more. I felt so blessed.

The party began and I said, "You may think you are ordinary people,
but in my book, you are extraordinary!" I was not just celebrating my life;
I was celebrating their lives as well. I am convinced that everyone whom
I've met came into my life for a reason and all of them helped me one way
or another on my journey. We shared some stories, enjoyed music, and we
sisters sang songs from the past, like "Work for the Night is Coming." I

felt honored having my youngest brother, and my sisters attend. I imagined my two oldest brothers smiling on us from above. We grew up together even though our experiences were very different. For me, it was a glorious celebration of life and memories. I know mother was smiling on us and probably singing in harmony with us from her Heaven.

Seventy is just a number and I will continue to convince myself that this is true! My mother lived to be eighty years old, and she never focused on numbers, let alone her physical challenges. She just lived life the best she knew how, kept the faith, stayed busy, and helped others. I want to be like that and practice being the person I was meant to be.

For all the challenges I encountered throughout life, I learned many lessons. Life has a way of reminding us of what really is important, what really counts, and to focus on the positive. When the going gets rough, we can start over and look at our situations with fresh eyes. Keeping positive people by my side, those who are nurturing and encouraging has helped me so much along the way. It is one thing to know, but another thing to practice and appreciate what you discover is really important to you.

I have a long list of lessons I've learned during these seventy years; here are a few that have kept me strong and sure-footed on my pathway: Never give up! Learn to be a better listener. Show empathy. Forgive and let go. Look for the good in each person and don't judge. Be gentle to yourself. Keep busy and give back. Never stop laughing. Keep the faith and walk the talk. Be thankful!

# Downsizing

*"The ability to simplify means to eliminate the unnecessary*
*so that the necessary may speak." -*Hans Hofmann

Sixteen years flew by quickly. Carlton retired from his work and one day asked, "So when are you planning to retire?" "Oh my," I said, "I don't know if I want to." I said, "I can't imagine but I know I have to 'face the music' and think more seriously about the next chapter." It was hard to believe we were now in our seventies and it was time for another season in life. With mixed emotions I was determined to accept another new experience. I truly loved living on this mountain with the beauty of trees and nature surrounding us. Carlton and I made many good memories here and we treasured our connection to nature in this special place. We enjoyed our neighborhood having wonderful and helpful people. To leave meant we were on yet another adventure, and once again making big adjustments.

We soon planned to downsize and put our Mountain Hideaway on the market. Downsizing meant getting rid of many things and learning to let go. I hired a wonderful lady whose business was to help people downsize. Oh, I knew how to organize but to get rid of things was overwhelming! She said, "Sandy, divide your things into five piles, one for donations, one for junk, one to recycle, and things to keep for your next place." I was supposed to ask myself, as I picked up each item, "Does this thing bring me joy?" "Do I need this anymore—if I didn't use it for a few years why am I hanging on to it?" She said, "And lastly, make sure you save the emotional things for last so you don't get too distracted." I thought, *And we can fill a bucket of tears and add that to the pile.*

And so this difficult process played out and Carlton and I did the best we could sorting. We reminisced about the items we had gotten on trips as souvenirs, things we had saved from our childhoods, toys we had saved that our daughters had played with. On and on it went, as we sorted through everything! Besides some of our personal things, we had to get rid of a lot of the operational and decoration items in the B&B as well. Intellectually I felt ready to make the change, but emotionally the tears of joy and sadness came and went like waves. For as many transitions as we had experienced in the course of our lives, I did not anticipate that this one would be so difficult, but for me it was. I thought to myself, *That was then, and this is now, and we will take strength from the fact that the Divine will continue to be with us.*

During 2017, we looked for another house closer to State College and finally sold our Mountain Hideaway home. We decided to rent for a year and build a place in Boalsburg, a little town 4 miles from State College. Finding a place among nature and being surrounded by the beautiful mountains was our priority. Indeed, we were blessed to find a beautiful spot with abundant forest covering the hills across from the house, which was at the outermost cul-de-sac in the neighborhood that stretched down towards town.

The very first year we were in our new home, we saw a beautiful bear with five cubs in our driveway. Deer roamed through our yard and wooded area and we saw and heard wild turkeys. I said to Carlton one day, "You know, I really think these animals followed us here from Mountain Hideaway." Gradually we adjusted to our lovely area where nature had no problem bringing us peace and joy. Home is where we are and it feels right. Are we finished downsizing, curtailing, and cutting back? No, but we continue to practice letting go and are much more awake about hoarding things. Shopping is fun but I try to think twice before I buy something. We try to focus more on giving back and less on buying things. For me, I can breathe easier, knowing that I have less stuff that I don't need. We are grateful each day for our home, nature, and for each other.

# Finding Balance During Retirement

*"Balance is the key to everything. What we do, think,
say, eat, feel, they all require awareness, and through this
awareness, we can grow."* ~Koi Fresco

When I was a child, I remember trying to balance myself as I walked across a narrow cement wall. When I got to the end, I felt so happy and relieved that I made it without falling. I also remember in gym class when I had to walk on the balance beam in front of my classmates. As long as I focused, carefully putting one foot in front of the other, I made it. The key was to focus, be steady, and follow through.

Carlton and I are now in the season of our lives called retirement. Along the way I heard many people talking about what it was like to be retired. Some were having the time of their lives and others were still finding their way. For me, retirement was hard to relate to and my guess is, it had to do with me growing up on the farm where working seemed to be second to sanctity. I don't remember hearing about the concept of retirement very often.

I've discovered that when I'm in harmony with everything around me and have a balanced life, it creates positive energy. Balance brings me joy and contentment when I feel in sync with the flow of life. It is different for each person, but it is essential to have and maintain. I will be the first to admit that this transition to retire was not easy for me. I always had a schedule and a routine. Retirement was like looking at a blank canvas, not knowing what to paint or how to begin. This felt unfamiliar to me but I was never one to give up. I had to find my way.

I remembered attending a workshop on "making transitions" about seventeen years ago. When I attended the class I had just started a new job and the transition went smoothly but I wanted to see what new things I could learn. Many in the class were retired people and they were all experiencing something different, adjusting to their transitions. Some of the people were struggling and others were having a great time. I realized then how much I enjoyed my work but if I ever got to that point and retired, I wanted to be prepared. It is funny how that works for me, to understand something intellectually, yet on another level experience the opposite, having all kinds of mixed emotions. I thought, *I have plenty of time and for now, no need to worry.* Funny how time slipped away so rapidly.

The time came when we were planning to downsize, sell our place, and look for another house as we entered retirement. That is a full plate of changes to think about. Downsizing meant sorting and letting go of things. Selling our place meant that we had to have the house in order and prepared for potential buyers. Finding another place took time and looking back, I see that the time leading up to retirement was one big adventure and not always easy. After we got settled in our new house, I earnestly made a list of priorities and focused on how I wanted to reinvent myself. I started visualizing what a balanced life looked like for this new season in life.

I wrote down my ideas and focused on my physical well-being, spiritual needs, and mental development. I wasn't afraid to reach out for advice and ask those who were ahead of me on this journey how they handled retirement. Over and over I heard, "You are not alone," and "Think about how many transitions we go through in a lifetime." How true, all through life we experience many changes. Carlton adjusted much more quickly than I did with the transitions. He was more ready than I was for retirement. Only I could decide what was best for me.

I continued to focus on my list of ideas and was willing to take more risks as I created balance in this new phase of life. The following are things that I enjoy and focus on:

- I decided I wanted to stay in contact with students so I began substitute teaching. It took courage at this age, but I had the attitude that if I didn't feel comfortable, or confident, I would not do it. Young people are an inspiration and can teach us a great deal.

- I decided to write a book, which was huge, because I never considered myself a writer, but I found that "everyone has a story, and everyone can write." That comment stayed with me as I attended several creative writing classes and I continue to work on improving my writing skills.
- I will continue to have my flower garden and enjoy nature. An awesome gift! Each year I make sure I have plenty of plants for pollinating. Bees, butterflies, and hummingbirds are a thrill to watch.
- I look forward to traveling more with Carlton as long as we are able.
- I enjoy volunteering and reaching out to help others.
- Focusing more on "mindfulness" has been very helpful but it takes tons of practice. It is amazing what can happen when we are awake and open to learning, no matter what age we are.
- Keeping people in my life who are encouraging, supportive, and positive has been a real bonus all my life. Staying connected is essential as we enter this twilight zone. After several of my friends and family members died, I realized how important it is to keep good people with me always.
- I've learned to value focusing on being kind to myself. It is empowering to like who we are. Dwelling on regrets, mistakes, and not forgiving ourselves can only bring negative energy.
- Faith, family, and friends are my inspiration.

In this season of life, I'm not walking across a balance beam, but I am keeping balanced by staying active and involved. Things are entirely different from when I was younger, of course, but I still need to plan and aim for a balanced life. As Dr. Seus said, "You have brains in your head. You have feet in your shoes. You can steer yourself any direction you choose."

# Home is Wherever I Am

*"Peace—that was the other name for home."*
~Kathleen Norris

Not too long ago, our grown daughters came home for a visit. My husband and I had just built our new home, which evolved into our 12th move and again we called it "Home Sweet Home." Still, we were in a new environment, a new community, and definitely feeling the sense of starting over yet again.

Before the girls left to return to their individual homes, they both brought their feelings to our attention, "You know this is not 'home' to us." They had grown up in another house in another community. I understood what they meant and acknowledged their feelings.

I thought about what they said many times and I began to realize that *home* might have many definitions. Is it possible that home is actually a state of mind? Maybe home does not have to be a place, but what we experience within us, not a place in the past, but more importantly, where we are in the present with ourselves.

There have been times when I felt I had to go back to where I grew up, whether physically or mentally or both. I remember sitting and pondering about the memories of home, both good and bad. But more importantly, I had to go full circle, back to my childhood with my adult perspectives in tow, to rediscover what I really experienced and what I was taught at home during my growing up years. I had to ask difficult questions and sort out what would be of value to me in the present moment.

*Sandra L. Miller*

The process was similar to when Carlton and I scaled down from Mountain Hideaway and moved to our smaller home in State College, and we had to sort through all of our possessions. But this thinking about home, I realized, was about sorting through memories, feelings, and sometimes beliefs, rather than things. After sorting through the negative and positive experiences of my life, I could decide what to save and hold dear for the present. During this reflection, I had to work through forgiveness and letting go, in order not to become stuck in the more challenging experiences of my life. And I do find this continues to be an ongoing process as life progresses.

Today, mostly I feel like I am home, having a feeling of peace within myself and enjoying simply, "what is." Home for me is not necessarily a place on the map or a house, but a special gift I give myself every day, of peace and contentment. We carry our homes with us wherever we go. The saying, "Home Sweet Home" can only be sweet if one has peace within. At this point, I realize *I* am home wherever I go.

274

# Living in Gratitude

*"Gratitude makes sense of our past, brings peace for today,*
*and creates a vision for tomorrow."* -Melody Beattie

When I flash back to when I was a very young child, I realize that that's when I first became aware of the concept of gratitude, as I sat right there, at the dinner table. Grace was said by one of us, "God is great, God is good, let us thank Him for our food...." When our parents prayed their prayers were longer, but always included "Thank you God for our many blessings" and they would have a list of things they were thankful for that changed from day to day. My journey of "living in gratitude" first began at home.

I learned about gratitude from both the good and the bad experiences of my life. At a very young age if I showed any signs of not liking a certain food, my mother would say, "Sandra, think of all the children who do not have enough to eat each day. We need to be thankful for this food." Or if I didn't like my new pair of shoes, or the color of my stockings, I would hear in the background my mother reciting part of a Bible verse, "In everything give thanks." I Thessalonians 5:18, King James Version. It is true, that I did not always give thanks in *all* things but I became aware of the importance of gratitude at an early age.

There were many sermons I heard in church about being thankful and the theme of gratitude continued to weave through all of my growing up years. I heard "Devote yourselves to prayer, being watchful and thankful." My child-like faith was kindled and it made an impression on me at least on a certain level of understanding. However, it is one thing to be taught something and another thing to really experience it from the heart.

The definition of *gratitude* is simple but full of meaning. Dictionary. com defines it as "the quality or feeling of being grateful or thankful." I remember the day my brother Karl had a farm accident and was in a coma for several days. My parents and friends prayed on a regular basis for his recovery. Fortunately, he survived and I can still hear it said over and over, "Isn't it wonderful that he came through it? We are so thankful." It was then that I realized that some of the things we are most grateful for are those that seem out of our control, yet we feel the presence of something larger than ourselves guiding our way. I am thankful for that presence in my life.

All the adventures and misadventures of my life have taught me many lessons, many of which came from the people who inspired me, like my teachers, my mother, my family, and good friends. When I was young, too often it was easier to dwell on the hurts, misfortunes, and unfairness of life. I had a little attitude surgery as I grew older, and learned to put life into perspective and focus on the positive. My mother never judged, but she was well aware of the contrast between abundance and poverty. I walked along with her when I was very young as she visited people at a mission in the city not far from where we lived on our farm, who had needs much greater than ours. Later she told me, "We are no better than anyone else, but we need to think how we can help others who are in need." Because of her loving stewardship, I became aware of the struggles of poverty at a young age and what we could do to help alleviate them. Though I didn't have a lot of possessions like some of my other friends, I knew that I always had enough. Through my mother's gentle lessons, I was taught how real and painful poverty is, and to be helpful to those who do not have enough food, clothing, medical care, and education. I believe that mother's lessons were a loving part of the reason that Carlton and I brought Inez into our family. And I am so thankful for the blessings she has brought to our lives. With our two daughters, we are keenly aware of the abundance in our lives, and so thankful for all we could do as parents, to provide for them.

When I was old enough to join my youth group, we were assigned to various projects with a focus on helping others. Whether it was delivering Christmas baskets of goodies to those who were confined to their homes, going to the prison to sing Christmas carols, or visiting elders in the convalescent homes, I became more aware of many ways I could help to ease their burdens or bring them joy, and I am thankful for the abundance in my life that has made it possible for me to do that. Those early experiences stuck with me and I am grateful for all of the people who inspired and encouraged me to see beyond the negative, focus on the positive, and be involved in activities that help to make the world a better place.

One of the most inspiring people I know of was Matthew Joseph Thaddeus Stepanek, whose challenges were great, and yet he never lost his faith or the love that filled his heart. Though he was born with a rare and serious disease, one that took the lives of all three of his siblings, his main goal in life was to inspire others. Amazing! As of this writing, his mother is still living with the same disease. Despite his many physical challenges, I find it so impressive that his thoughts were always of others and his heart was filled with love for the whole world.

Even though Mattie was so young, he became a widely known motivational speaker and advocate for peace. He wrote several books, including *Heartsongs,* and *Loving through Heartsongs.* He chose those titles because he believed that the inspiring messages that he wrote down originated from God, and he called them his "heartsongs." He believed that every person has their own heartsongs. Mattie was a saint and an inspiring example of being thankful no matter what he encountered. He reached out to everyone and blessed us through his example. His message of hope is a great reminder for each of us. Mattie died in June 2004 at the age of thirteen, and his legacy lives on through the Mattie J. T. Stepanek Foundation, which continues to spread his message of peace, hope, and love throughout the world.

As I reflect on what it means to "live in gratitude," I realize that the concept has a different meaning for me now that I'm in this new season of life. What I know for sure is that it is never too late to show gratitude and I've found that it changes my outlook on most everything! I am reminded to put the challenges and blessings of my life into perspective and be thankful for what I have and what I'm able to do!

Living in gratitude is a constant reminder for me to be thankful for all those life lessons of the past that enrich my appreciation of living in the present moment. Thanks to those teachers who encouraged and believed in me. I'm grateful that I found the courage to pursue my dreams. I am thrilled to have achieved them, and to have encouraged others along the way. Thanks to my friends who said, "You go girl," cheering me on and coaching me to never give up. I will be forever grateful for my dear mother who shared her faith and her giving heart with those around her. She quietly gave me her blessing for the goals I wanted to achieve in life. And for our daughters and my siblings who bounced along listening, laughing, and always saying, "You can do it." Always, huge thanks go to my husband who saw the good in life no matter how tough things were at times. He knew what it was like to study hard and accomplish his goals. They all deserve a crown of gold! I know now, that living in gratitude brings joy, not just to myself, but to others.

## PART SIX

# Tribute to Mother

# Mother's Generosity

*"You give but little when you give of your possessions. It is
when you give of yourself that you truly give."*
~Kahlil Gibran

When I was young, I often heard my mother ask, "Remember what the Bible says about giving?" Even before getting the dictionary to share the definition of what giving means, my mother would share a verse like, "It's better to give than receive," Acts 20:35 King James Version, and 2 Corinthians 9:6-7 "God loves a cheerful giver." She said, "There are at least 21 Bible verses about giving." The Bible was her road map and of course it left an impression on me. I saw firsthand my mother's quality of kindness and generosity in the way she lived her life and gave to others.

When my mother returned from visiting us in Bolivia, South America, she decided to do something different again. She was in new territory living by herself and now was in her mid 60s. I never heard her complain, but one day she said, "I really would like to do more for others and give back while I can." Our family gave her our blessings as Mother began to apply for different service opportunities. She was thrilled to be able to help with charities, whether it was making knotted blankets, providing food, or making monetary donations. She wrote the family lovely letters, some in poetry form, and shared how she enjoyed the work. We were happy for her. And Mother was happy because she was doing what she had told us was important in life, giving back to others.

The act of giving rubbed off on me and my husband. When we were children, we were each given a little tin bank shaped like a globe, the outside depicting all the geographical regions of the world. The church leaders asked us to save our money and fill the bank. They would show us on our small globes where the money would go—often to other countries—and we learned where they were located by studying the map on our little globes. On a given Sunday, we were asked to bring the banks to church and the money was collected and given to a special charity.

Anytime someone at church or in our community became ill or for those who were homebound, it was a common practice for others to help provide meals and visit. I remember sitting with the adults as they visited people; sometimes they sang and prayed for those who were experiencing challenges. Mother was loved for her kindness and her giving spirit.

Taking part in the offerings at church and visiting people who were sick or needed help made an impression on me at a young age. I found it rewarding to help when I could. Later, when I was a young teenager, our church encouraged the young people to participate with charitable projects. I found giving rewarding and learned many lessons about myself and others.

I remember a guest at Mountain Hideaway mentioning to me one time, "You know Sandy, you are so good with giving to others but you are not a good receiver." I was glad she reminded me because I think that verse "It is better to give than receive" was so ingrained in my mind that I had to learn that both are equally important! Giving is rewarding and I know my mother loved being generous. Her legacy lives on because she showed us how to reach out and help others.

As I've grown older, I realize that in learning to receive, there is a hidden gift. We are giving someone else the chance to experience giving. This is grace itself. We cannot give to others who are not willing to receive, so I work to embrace these two aspects of giving. I know how good it feels for me to be able to give to others, whether it's my time, knowledge, teaching, love, protection, encouragement, or more tangible things. I realize that my 70th birthday party was all about the celebration of both giving and receiving in my life. And for both I am very grateful.

Giving comes in many forms and I am always amazed when I think how my mother gave to others all her life. It might have been making a homemade cooked meal for a stranger or sharing with our neighbors. We loved how she did what she could as long as possible. Her positive and loving spirit lives on forever!

# Saying Goodbye to Mother

*"Generosity is the most natural outward expression of an*
*inner attitude of compassion and loving-kindness."*
~Dalai Lama XIV

When I was young, death was far from my mind and maybe subconsciously I thought my mother would live forever. As I grew older and began to have my own life, thankfully she was still living, but I was so busy, I didn't take the time for her as often as I could have. I wondered *Did I take her life for granted?* She and I did not have a bad relationship but I wasn't always easy, and we were not always close.

I was probably in my thirties when I realized it was important for me to reconnect and get to know my mother better. My mother was not the same when I was young as when I grew older, into adulthood. She changed, like we all do, and later, after her children were grown, she seemed to try to find herself again in new ways. Mother became a young widow when she was in her 50s. She was ready for new experiences, and she took advantage of opportunities that came her way. She stepped out of her comfort zone for adventure and new experiences.

As time went on, we visited more often and we built a closer relationship. One of the things we really enjoyed together was playing Scrabble. She was really good with words and many times won. We both loved nature and always enjoyed sitting outside on the porch, listening to the birds sing, and watching them. If I shared a worry, she would say, "I often think of that verse in Matthew 6:26, King James Version. "Behold the fowls of the air: for they sow not, neither do they reap, nor gather into barns; yet your heavenly Father feedeth them. Are ye not much better than they?" I said, "Yes Mother, I do remember that verse, and I too, am amazed at how often we worry for nothing."

We were so happy that Mother continued to enjoy life while she was able. When she was in her early sixties she announced to the family, "My doctor told me I have to be put on a dialysis machine because my kidneys are both failing." We were all saddened but tried to be supportive the best we knew how.

Mother was on this treatment for seven years. She did everything she could: followed the doctor's orders, took her prescribed pills along with some supplements, and prayed for healing. The family was told that she would never get off of the dialysis machine, but my mother stuck to her beliefs.

After six years, Mother told the doctor that she was feeling much better and would like to be put on the machine for fewer hours. We think he was more than surprised when she told him this, but she kept insisting that she would like to try it. The doctor said, "Okay Barbara, we will try it, but you know that this is not typical." I'm thinking, *Oh ye of little faith, Mother is not typical.* Sure enough, she continued on the machine for fewer hours, and she said she was feeling better. Later, she told the doctor, "I'm really feeling much better and I would like to go off of the machine entirely." Again, she surprised the doctor with her request. He paused and said, "You know Barbara, this is not typical; actually, it is unheard of." Mother smiled and again insisted that she would like to try. So, the doctor let her try it and through a miracle, she stayed off of the machine for the rest of her life!

During the years while she was on dialysis, a male friend was pursuing her to go out to eat and spend time together in between her dialysis sessions. She wasn't sure what to do about it for a long time and was concerned about how her family would feel. When she gathered the family together and shared, we said, "Mother, this is totally up to you and we want you to be happy." This would be her decision. We knew this man, and felt very comfortable if she wanted to follow through. Well, she did follow through and began dating the man. Later, my mother married him, and they had ten wonderful years together. In fact, on their tenth anniversary, our families pooled together and gave them a gift certificate to go on a trip to Europe to see Switzerland where their ancestors are from. My mother was overwhelmed; she cried happy tears. My stepdad couldn't believe it and was very appreciative.

Shortly after they returned from their trip, on a Sunday afternoon, my stepdad was resting on the sofa while my mother was playing the piano in their living room. My stepdad started coughing and Mother quickly stopped playing to check on him. She knew something was wrong and immediately called 911. By the time the Emergency Medical Services unit arrived, my stepdad had died of a heart attack. Once again, my mother was a widow. Our whole family grieved with her, knowing how much she would miss him. She was a real trooper and did the best she could in the days that followed.

We were fortunate to have Mother with us for nine more years after our stepdad died. My sisters and I often took Mother on surprise trips for weekends. It was so much fun to be with her. She seemed to enjoy the adventures and many times we saw her youthful side. It didn't take much for all of us to have some good laughs at the simplest things on these trips. She would say, "Oh girls, remember the time on the farm when..." and then we'd laugh again. We often say today, "What great memories we made with her!"

During the last days of her life, we sat by her bedside and tried to comfort her as she gradually slipped away. It was painful to see her struggle and suffer and all we could do was hold her hand and tell her that we loved her. We told her many times. We siblings and other family members took turns being with her as she faded into her heavenly home. She died on January 16, 1997.

We will not remember Mother as we saw her those last days but we will remember her as the woman of great courage and love which she truly showed us throughout her life. Mother loved her children. She loved when we all sang together. She loved her grandchildren and enjoyed playing with them. She never stopped praying for each of us children and grandchildren.

We will remember how Mother kept her faith in God, loved music, loved traveling, and lived life to the fullest. Her spirit is with us and we'll always remember her generosity! We carry and express the best that she instilled in us as we continue in our life journeys.

## PART SEVEN

# Mother's Poetry

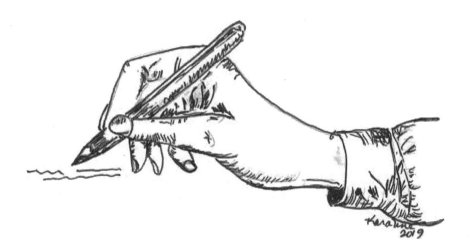

# This House

## ~Barbara M. Hauck

Bless this house dear Lord above
With happiness and with Thy love.

Bless the door that opens wide
To the warmth that waits inside.

Touch its windows with Thy Light
Be its comfort in the night.

Grant its peace and sweet accord
Make this home Thy home, dear Lord.

# On and On with Him

~Barbara M. Hauck

Precious Lord, I need your Hand as I move on
From these dear friends to those unknown.

To scenes and places, I've never been
Thou art my fortress, my strength, my battles to win.

Such Love so amazing and never to end
I am humbled, I marvel to have such a Friend.

I rejoice in His wonders and mercies to me
And glad to tell others, from sin He sets free.

To love and to serve Him, no matter where
To sing His praises and His good news share.

When thinking of you, then I will pray
Be it nighttime or through the course of the day.

Many joys and blessings, rest upon each one of you
Jesus' help is always present, His Love is ever True.

# Surrounded by Nature

~Barbara M. Hauck

The roses are wild, but mosquitoes seem tame
They fly so slow, act like they're lame!

The birds, some are big, like the raven for one
He flaps his big wings until the set of the sun.

Then wee Jenny wren, how sweetly she sings
To all who will hear her, much happiness brings.

# Things in Common

~Barbara M. Hauck

Mary and I, they say we are a pair
I guess it's because we have much to share.

About things like, what's good to eat,
How to bake bread or how to do the meat.

The easy quick way to fold the towels
To fold the sheets, there are many styles.

She loves the roses, and so do I
Today she brought me one, and it near made me cry.

So sweet was her thought and the rose it was pink
I placed it in a cup with water to drink.

We often remark about the work of God's Hand
Everything is so beautiful on lake or on land.

# Bolivia

~Barbara M. Hauck

Getting around by bus, truck or jeep
Seeing many cattle horses and sheep.
Very high mountains and dry riverbeds
Small mud brick houses and wee tiny sheds.
...This is Bolivia!

People from valleys and the highlander too
Some wearing sandals, not many a shoe.
Much land is a tangle of vine and tree
Plenty of wildflowers, and some gardens you see.
...Here in Bolivia!

The women of Highlands wear a black derby hat
Those of the valley, are high, white, and flat.
Their back burdened down with a babe or food
Or vegetables for market or some fire wood.
...It's life in Bolivia.

The men of the Mountains wear black hats too
Often leading a donkey, very little they do.
It is sights like this you see in traveling around
In Bolivia's culture they are commonly found.
...Unforgettable Bolivia.

# That Mountain

## ~Barbara M. Hauck

Here in Phoenix as I look to the east
I see a mountain shaped just like a beast.

The Camelback it's called, an appropriate name
Its size and its beauty give it much fame.

Many lessons I see as I look there
The monk on its face like it's bowing in prayer.

Seems the camel is heavily burdened down
Like some living here and in the world around.

There is help for us all when things aren't right
God's ready to lift burdens and make the heart light.

# Precious Lord

~Barbara M. Hauck

Let me live for Thee
Let me give for Thee
Let me walk for Thee
Let me talk for Thee
Let me be for Thee
At rest on Thy breast. Amen

# Gratitude

~Barbara M. Hauck


Praise God You save, keep and satisfy
Your words are Truth and my needs You do supply.

I come to You now with the thanks I owe
Springs of joy in my heart continually flow.

Your love is so tender and there I abide
My shelter and haven the safe place to hide.

As on this journey together we go
It's so pleasant Lord because it's You I know.

# Good Morning Lord!

## ~Barbara M. Hauck

Good Morning Dear Lord, it's such a lovely day!
So happy You are right by and never away.

Lest I who would wander and gad about
Resulting then in vexation and doubt.

The light of the sun, placed there by your will
Adds more to the day than a vitamin pill.

Lord in these hours of light, there is much to be done
Daily tasks in the house and errands to run.

Please precious Lord, help me keep still!
And not rush about, thus causing a spill.

So thankful Lord, You always Love and You care
You forgive when I err, You are ever so fair.

# Talking to and Thinking of God

~Barbara M. Hauck

Today Lord as I face each test
Strengthen me to do my best,
That I may in Thy strength be strong
Then praise and thank Thee all day long.

Thy goodness, peace, and joy, and care
There's none like Thee, none to compare.
Living for time and things that we see
Soon they will pass, no more to be.

The great satisfaction in life, is when we
Look to our Maker depend wholly on Thee.
The Creator, who formed us out of the dust
In Him alone, it is safe to trust.

Men today keep seeking fame and for things
Get all tied up like a ball of string.
So, wrapped and tangled, they forget to prepare
To make sure their names are written "up there."

God wants to keep and Father us all
It's up to us to answer His call.
His arm is outstretched to take us in
He's longing to pardon and forgive all our sin.

# In Everything

~Barbara M. Hauck

Thank Thee God for everything
Times of sadness, times to sing.
Thanks for Love so warm and deep
With tender constant watch doth keep.
Thanks for Hope to see thy face
For Peace and Joy and Saving Grace.

# Love Everlasting

~Barbara M. Hauck

As I stopped and waited for the light to turn green
It was then I noticed an unusual scene.

Down the street in the wind blew a paper cup lid
On its edge it rolled, between traffic it hid.

I thought of the danger in which it was in
Like man being tossed by the forces of sin.

This world has many attractions to turn us aside
But all praises to God in His Love and Care I safely abide.

# Talk at 2 a.m.

## ~Barbara M. Hauck

The hours of the day have come to an end
It's deep in the night and I'll talk to my Friend.
Lord, I'm so glad You are with me always
You hear my thanks and my needs as I pray.
Sleep nor drowsiness never come in Your eye
It is on Your Love and Your Care I can always rely.
Though times may bring many changes about
With You it's not so, so why should I doubt?
I pray for my Loved ones, Lord I claim
That they all see Thee, and own Your Dear Name.
As the "grands" grow up, may they heed your call
Willing in service great or small.

# Lone Shoe

## ~Barbara M. Hauck

I drove to work east on route number thirty
On the road lay a shoe cold and dirty.

How it got there and to whom did it belong?
The shoe it was good, but the place it was wrong.

I thought as I prayed for the one who once wore it
Oh God may his heart with Thy Love be close knit.

Items scattered many times I see by the way
At one time belonging to some soul and it's for them I pray.

## PART EIGHT

# Mother's Favorite Recipes

## Potato Soup with Celery and Eggs

| | |
|---|---|
| 2 cups diced potatoes | 3 hard-cooked eggs, chopped |
| 1 medium-sized onion | 1 quart milk |
| 1/4 cup celery | 1 tablespoon chopped parsley |
| 2 tablespoons butter | Salt and pepper |

Boil diced potatoes and onions together in 3 cups of water.
Add 1 teaspoon salt.
Add chopped celery when potatoes are partially cooked.
When potatoes are soft, pour in heated milk and add chopped eggs.
Add parsley and butter just before serving.
Serves 4.

Mrs. J. Irvin Lehman - Chambersburg, Pa.
From *Mennonite Community Cookbook*, 65th Anniversary Edition (p. 40).
(Herald Press, 2015) Used with permission. www.HeraldPress.com

## Grandma's Milk or Rivel Soup

| | |
|---|---|
| 2 quarts milk | 1 1/2 teaspoons salt |
| 1 cup flour* | 2 to 3 tablespoons cream |
| 1 large egg* | |
| 1/4 cup of milk* | |

Heat milk to boiling point in top of double boiler. Add salt.

To make rivels, rub egg and flour together, then add 1/4 cup milk. These are best made by cutting through mixture with two forks. Drop rivels, which are no larger than a cherry stone, into the boiling milk stirring to prevent packing together.*

Keep milk at boiling point for 3 to 5 minutes.

Serves 6 to 8.

Mrs. Curtis C. Cressman, New Hamburg, Ont., Can.

From *Mennonite Community Cookbook*, 65th Anniversary Edition (p. 48). (Herald Press, 2015) Used with permission. www.HeraldPress.com

*Rivel Instruction Mrs. Andrew Beller, Castorland, N. Y.

From *Mennonite Community Cookbook*, 65th Anniversary Edition (p. 40). (Herald Press, 2015) Used with permission. www.HeraldPress.com

## Chicken Potpie

1 chicken, preferably a 4-pound hen
1 teaspoon salt
Water to cover
4 medium-sized potatoes, sliced
2 tablespoon minced parsley

For potpie dough:

2 cups flour
1/2 teaspoon salt
2 eggs
2-3 tablespoons water
1 tablespoon shortening

Cut chicken into serving pieces, cover with water and cook until tender.
Season with salt.
When chicken is almost soft, add the sliced potatoes.
Add squares of potpie dough and cook 20 more minutes.

To make potpie dough, make a well in the flour and add the eggs and salt.
Work together into a stiff dough; if too dry add water or milk.
Roll out the dough as thin as possible (1/8 inch) and cut in 1-inch squares
    with a knife or pastry wheel.
Drop into the boiling broth, which should be sufficient to cover the
    chicken well. Cook 10-12 minutes.
Add the chopped parsley.
Serves 6 to 8.

Mrs. Harvey M. Stover, Souderton, Pa.; Mrs. J. C. Clemens, Lansdale, Pa.,
    Mrs. Amos Kreider, East Petersburg, Pa.
From *Mennonite Community Cookbook*, 65th Anniversary Edition (pp. 96-
    97). (Herald Press, 2015) Used with permission. www.HeraldPress.com

## Pot Roast ~Barbara M. Hauck

3 1/2-pound chuck roast
1 teaspoon of salt per pound
1 teaspoon pepper
1/2 cup flour
2 tablespoons butter or olive oil
1/2 cup hot tomato juice or water
2 small onions, sliced
8 medium potatoes, peeled, cut in half
8 carrots, peeled, cut in half
Handful of minced parsley

Rub salt and pepper into meat and coat the roast with flour.
Brown meat and onion in 2 tablespoons butter or olive oil until seared on
    all sides.
Place meat in roasting pan or in casserole dish.
Surround the meat with onions, potatoes and carrots.
Add hot tomato juice or water.
Cover and bake at 350° for 3 hours.
Sprinkle parsley on top when ready to serve.
Serves 6.

## Cole Slaw ~Barbara M. Hauck

4 cups finely shredded green cabbage (raw)
1/2 cup of shredded carrots (raw)
1/2 teaspoon celery seed
1/4 cup sour cream
1/4 cup vinegar
3 tablespoons sugar
1 teaspoon salt
1/3 teaspoon prepared mustard

Chop or shred the cabbage.
Mix together the sugar, salt, celery seed, mustard, vinegar, and sour cream.
Pour over cabbage and mix well.
Chill at least 30 minutes before serving.
Serves 6.

## Macaroni Salad ~Barbara M. Hauck

Cook 1 pound of elbow macaroni, drain off water and rinse in cold water.
Add 1/2 cup of diced celery.

Add 1 tablespoon diced onion, dash of parsley, 1 grated carrot and 4 chopped, hard boiled eggs.

# Potato Salad ~Barbara M. Hauck

6 cups of cooked Idaho or russet potatoes, skinned and cut into small
   pieces
1/4 cup onions, minced
1 cup celery cut into small pieces
1/2 cup of shredded carrots
1 1/2 teaspoon salt
1/2 teaspoon pepper
1/4 cup chopped parsley
4 chopped, hard boiled eggs

# Dressing: (Can be used for Macaroni or Potato Salad)

1/2 cup sugar
1 tablespoon cornstarch
1 teaspoon dry mustard
3/4 cup water
2 beaten eggs
1/2 tablespoon salt
Pinch of pepper
1/2 cup vinegar

Combine the above and cook over medium heat until bubbly and thickened. Stir occasionally.
Cool, cover surface with plastic wrap. When completely cooled, stir in 3/4 cup of mayonnaise.

Pour dressing over macaroni salad or potato salad and mix gently.

## Seven-Day Sweet Pickles

| | |
|---|---|
| 7 pounds medium-sized cucumbers | 8 cups sugar |
| Water to cover | 2 tablespoons salt |
| 1 quart vinegar | 2 tablespoons mixed pickle spices |

Wash cucumbers and cover them with boiling water.
Let stand 24 hours and drain.
Repeat each day for 4 days, using fresh water each time.
On the fifth day, cut cucumbers in 1/4 inch rings.
Combine vinegar, sugar, salt and spices.
Bring liquid to a boil and pour over sliced cucumbers.
Let stand 24 hours.
Drain syrup and bring to a boil.
Pour over cucumbers.
Repeat on the sixth day.
On the last day, drain off the syrup again and bring it to a boil.
Add cucumber slices and bring to the boiling point.
Pack into hot jars and seal.
These are very crisp and delicious pickles.

Mrs. Samuel Nafziger, Kalona, Iowa
From *Mennonite Community Cookbook*, 65th Anniversary Edition
(p. 407). (Herald Press, 2015) Used with permission. www.
HeraldPress.com

*Sandra L. Miller*

## Old-Fashioned Apple Dumplings

**Sauce:**

6 medium-sized baking apples  2 cups brown sugar

2 cups flour  2 cups water

2 1/2 teaspoons baking powder  1/4 cup butter

1/2 teaspoon salt  1/4 teaspoon cinnamon or nutmeg (optional)

2/3 cup shortening

1/2 cup milk


Pare and core apples. Leave whole.

To make pastry, sift flour, baking powder and salt together,

Cut in shortening until particles are about the size of small peas.

Sprinkle milk over mixture and press together lightly, working dough only
enough to hold together.

Roll dough as for pastry and cut into 6 squares and place an apple on each.

Fill cavity in apple with sugar and cinnamon.

Pat dough around apple to cover it completely.

Fasten edges securely on top of apple.

Place dumplings 1 inch apart in a greased baking pan.


Pour over them the sauce made as follows:


Combine brown sugar, water and spices.

Cook for 5 minutes, remove from heat and add butter.


Bake at 350° for 35 to 40 minutes.

Baste occasionally during baking.

Serve hot with rich milk or cream.


Mrs. Forrest Ogburn, Dallastown, Pa.; Mrs. U. Grant Weaver, Johnstown,
Pa.; Mrs. James Bauman, Oyster Point, Va.

From *Mennonite Community Cookbook*, 65th Anniversary Edition (pp.
309-310). (Herald Press, 2015) Used with permission. www.
HeraldPress.com

# Cherry Pie

| | |
|---|---|
| 2 1/2 cups sour cherries | 3 tablespoons minute tapioca |
| 1/3 cup cherry juice | 1 tablespoon butter |
| 1/3 cup brown sugar | 1/3 teaspoon almond extract |
| 1/3 cup granulated sugar | Pastry for 2 (9 inch) crusts* |

Combine cherries, juice, sugars, flavoring and tapioca.
Let stand 15 minutes.
Pour into pastry-lined pie plate. Dot with butter.
Place crust or strips on top as preferred.
Bake at 425° for 10 minutes, then in moderate oven (375°) for 30 minutes.
Makes 1 (9 inch) pie.

Mrs. Fannie A. L. Gable, York, Pa.; Mrs. Ira Eigsti, Buda, Ill.
From *Mennonite Community Cookbook*, 65th Anniversary Edition (pp. 364-365). (Herald Press, 2015) Used with permission. www. HeraldPress.com

## *Pastry (for 9-inch double-crust pie)

| | |
|---|---|
| 2 1/4 cups flour | 1/2 teaspoon salt |
| 2/3 cup shortening | 1/3 cup cold water |

Combine flour and salt in a mixing bowl.

Cut shortening into flour with a pastry blender or two knives.

Do not overmix; these are sufficiently blended when particles are the size of peas.

Add water gradually, sprinkling 1 tablespoon at a time over mixture.

Toss lightly with a fork until all particles of flour have been dampened.

Use only enough water to hold the pastry together when it is pressed between the fingers. It should not feel wet.

Roll dough into a round ball, handling as little as possible.

Roll out on a lightly floured board into a circle 1/8 inch thick and 1 inch larger than the diameter of the top of the pan.

From *Mennonite Community Cookbook*, 65th Anniversary Edition (pp. 354-355). (Herald Press, 2015) Used with permission. www. HeraldPress.com

# Red Chocolate Cake

**First Part:**

1/2 cup sugar
2/3 cup cocoa
1/2 cup water

Mix together and bring to boiling point. Cool.

**Second Part:**

| | |
|---|---|
| 1/2 cup shortening | 1 teaspoon soda |
| 1 cup sugar | 1/2 teaspoon salt |
| 2 eggs | 1/2 cup water |
| 2 cups cake flour | 1 teaspoon vanilla |

Cream shortening.
Add sugar gradually and beat until fluffy.
Add eggs and beat thoroughly.
Sift flour; measure and add salt and soda. Sift again.
Add sifted dry ingredients alternately with water and vanilla.
Combine with first mixture.
Pour into greased layer pans.
Bake at 350° for 30 minutes
Makes 2 (8 inch) layers.
A delicious cake.

Mrs. Alice Schrock, Tiskilwa, Ill.
From *Mennonite Community Cookbook*, 65th Anniversary Edition (pp. 207-208). (Herald Press, 2015) Used with permission. www.HeraldPress.com

*Sandra L. Miller*

## Mother's Caramel Icing ~Barbara M. Hauck

1 cup brown sugar
1/2 cup butter or margarine
1/4 cup milk, mix and boil 2 minutes
Cool and add 10x sugar, enough for a smooth icing

# Drop Sand Tarts ~Barbara M. Hauck

1 1/2 cups sugar
1 cup melted butter
2 eggs
2 1/2 cups sifted flour
1/2 teaspoon baking soda

Mix eggs, sugar and butter, then add flour and baking soda.
Drop by 1/2 teaspoon on greased cookie sheet and sprinkle with cinnamon
and sugar.

Bake at 350° 10 minutes

# Maple Drop Cookies ~Barbara M. Hauck

1 egg (beaten)
1/2 cup soft butter
1/2 cup maple syrup
1 1/2 cups flour
1/2 teaspoon baking soda
1/2 teaspoon salt
Walnuts, (optional)

Heat oven to 325°. Mix in bowl, egg, butter, syrup.
Sift flour, add baking soda and salt, and mix with the egg, butter and syrup.
Drop by teaspoon on greased baking sheet.
Bake 8 minutes. Yields 2 dozen.

# Fresh Peach Cobbler ~Barbara M. Hauck

**Step 1**

Slice 2 cups peaches, stir in 3/4 cup sugar and let stand.

**Step 2**

Place 3/4 or 1 stick butter or margarine in a deep baking dish, set in warm oven to melt.

**Step 3**

Mix a batter of 1 cup sugar, 3/4 cup flour and 2 teaspoons baking powder, pinch of salt, and 3/4 cup milk. Pour batter over melted butter or margarine and don't stir. Place peaches on top. Don't stir.
Bake 1 hour at 350°. Batter will rise to the top, it will be crisp and brown. Can be served with ice cream.

## Meadow Tea ~Sandra L. Miller

Meadow tea is a beverage that is made from a number of different types of mint, depending on personal preference. It's also known as "woolly leaf balsam and spearmint tea." If you decide to pick fresh leaves, be sure of the type of plant you're picking, and choose plants free of chemicals. When I was growing up, we could pick these mint leaves along streams and wooded areas on our farmland, and today, many people choose to grow them in their gardens.

After gathering or purchasing the leaves, wash them thoroughly in water. Heat a large kettle of water to boiling point, (2/3 full of water) and then turn off burner. Drop the clean mint leaves in and push them down in the water to submerge. It varies, with how many stems you want, 10 to 12 stems about 14 inches long and nicely covered with leaves is usually plenty. Keep in water for 30 minutes or less depending on how strong you like it. Strain tea through a strainer into a pitcher. Add lemon if desired. Use maple syrup, honey, or sugar to sweeten to taste.

## PART NINE

# Mountain Hideaway Recipes

## To-Die-For French Toast

1/4 cup butter or margarine
1/2 cup packed light brown sugar
1 tablespoon honey
2 tart apples, peeled and sliced (mix tart and gala apples)
Other fruits may be used for this recipe

1/2 loaf French sliced bread, or whole wheat, cut each slice of bread in half
2 whole eggs
3/4 cup milk
3/4 teaspoon pure vanilla extract

The night before you plan to serve this dish, melt the butter in a small saucepan or microwave. Stir in the brown sugar and syrup and stir until blended. Spread this mixture onto the bottom of a 13 x 9 inch nonstick baking pan, (if you use a glass baking dish, grease with butter). Spread apple slices evenly over the sugar mixture. Arrange bread slices over apple slices.

In a medium bowl, beat eggs until light and beat in milk and vanilla. Pour egg mixture evenly over bread. Cover with plastic wrap and refrigerate overnight.

In the morning, preheat the oven to 350°. Unwrap the dish and bake about 40 minutes or until the bread is golden brown. Remember not to turn on the cleaning button!
Makes 4 to 6 servings

Attributed to former innkeeper Peter Needham, The Buttonwood Inn on Mount Surprise in North Conway, New Hampshire. Used with permission.

# Baked Oatmeal ~Sandra L. Miller

3/4 cup of oil
1 1/2 cups of brown sugar
3 eggs
1 teaspoon salt
3 teaspoons baking powder
4 1/2 cups of oatmeal
1 1/2 cups of milk
1/4 cup honey

Mix all ingredients and put in 9 x 12 pan (glass baking dish).
Bake at 350° for 40 minutes.
After it is served people can pour milk over the warm oatmeal and top it
off with blueberries, peaches, or strawberries.

## Artichoke Cheese Oven Omelet

3/4 cup salsa
1 can (14 oz.) water-packed artichoke hearts, drained and chopped.
1 cup (4 oz.) shredded Monterey Jack cheese
1 cup (4 oz.) shredded cheddar cheese
1/4 cup grated parmesan cheese
6 eggs, beaten
1 cup (8 oz.) sour cream

Chopped fresh tomatoes, sliced ripe olives, minced chives, and minced onions, optional.

Spread salsa in a greased 9-inch, deep dish pie plate or baking dish. Top with the artichoke hearts and cheeses. In a bowl, whisk the eggs and sour cream. Pour over the cheeses. Bake, uncovered, at 350 degrees for 25-30 minutes or until a knife inserted near the center comes out clean. Let stand for 5 minutes before cutting. Garnish with tomatoes, olives, chives, and onions if desired.
Serves 6-8

## Breakfast Casserole with Vegetables

1 - 10 oz. pkg. chopped broccoli, thawed and drained or use fresh
4 ounces fresh mushrooms, sliced, (or from can, drained)
2 or 3 carrots grated or 1/2 bag of shredded carrots
1 large onion
1 cup of minced celery
1/2 stick of butter
Salt and pepper to taste

12 to 14 oz. Havarti cheese, grated (or mild cheddar)
6 to 7 large eggs
1/2 pint heavy cream

Sauté carrots, onion, and mushrooms in butter. Add broccoli and heat
through.

Grease quiche (deep) dish or other glass container.
Put vegetable mixture in bottom of dish. Top with cheese.

Beat eggs just to mix. Add cream to eggs and beat lightly.
Pour cream/egg mixture over vegetables. Use fork to lift vegetables and get
cream to bottom as well as on top.

Bake in preheated 350° oven for 1 hour or more.
Insert knife to check if center is finished. (Finished when nothing sticks
to knife.)
Serves 6 to 8.

# Hash Brown Quiche ~Sandra L. Miller

1-24 oz. package of hash browns, thawed
1/3 cup melted butter
1 cup shredded mild cheddar cheese
1/4 cup minced onions
1/4 cup minced celery
1 cup diced cooked ham or Canadian bacon
1/2 cup milk
2 large eggs
1/4 teaspoon salt

Preheat oven to 425°. Grease a 9-inch pie pan or baking dish.
Press hash browns into pan to form crust. Brush with melted butter. Bake
    25 minutes. Reduce oven temperature to 350 degrees.
Fill crust with cheese, ham and minced veggies. Whisk together milk, eggs,
    and seasoned salt. Pour in to pan and bake 30-40 minutes or until
    knife inserted in center comes out clean.
Serves 6.

(You may buy frozen hash browns with or without the onions and peppers
    or make your own hash browns if you already have a favorite recipe.)

## Breakfast Casserole

8 eggs, beaten
2 cups milk
3/4 teaspoon dry mustard
Salt and pepper to taste
1 can Cream of Mushroom Soup
1 cup cheddar cheese
6-8 slices bread

"Refrigerate at least overnight. Can be refrigerated for several days. We serve in individual ramekins and give guests a choice of precooked meats and vegetables they would like added to the casserole before baking."

"After adding meats and vegetables start in microwave on high setting for 2 minutes and 30 seconds. Transfer to 350 degree oven for another 10-15 minutes."

From Gary Anderson, created for The LandMark Inn at the Historic Bank of Oberlin, Kansas. Used with permission.

# Acknowledgments

First of all, thank you, dear readers, for your interest in my book. *Teachable Moments* evolved as I reflected on my life and started writing my stories. My hope is that you have found humor and inspiration as you accompanied me on my journey. I believe life is what we make it and I'm convinced we are here to help each other.

I would like to thank my wonderful husband Carlton, for listening to my ideas, reading early drafts of my stories and, giving me encouragement not to give up. He often took the time to discuss some of our past experiences, to share what he remembered, which was extra helpful. Funny how we each remembered different things about different events. He is the person who has always believed in me and I will forever be indebted to his commitment. Thank you, Dearie!

I would like to thank our two daughters, Ilisa and Inez, who brought us so much joy. I learned a lot from watching them grow up, become independent, and find their way in life. They have inspired me as I've watched them use their gifts to grow into the people they were meant to be.

Thanks to my wonderful siblings, Dolores, Yvonne, Delmar, and Dawn. They have always encouraged me to keep on going. They have been so helpful in remembering so many of the details of our stories. Thanks too, to David and Karl. I'm sure if they were here, they would also be cheering me on, as they always had in life.

A huge thanks to Ruth Ann Kulp, my friend that I met in a bookstore over forty years ago. We stood in the aisle and talked non-stop about what we were doing with our lives. We have stayed connected and encouraged each other along the way ever since. Ruth Ann is a talented musician, poet, and artist. We inspire each other as we continue to share our joy in being creative.

Thanks to Karl E. Leitzel, a talented artist who works in many media. He is a photographer, painter, and designer of beautiful signs for businesses. Many thanks to Karl for his design of the cover of my book, and for the photos of Kara and me. Thank you for working with us and sharing your creative talents, Karl.

I discovered writing a book is very challenging but rewarding at the same time. I could not have accomplished this project without the help of my outstanding editor, Jennifer Berghage. She is one of the most talented persons I've ever met as an editor, an artist, and a writer. I will forever be indebted to her expertise, insights, and feedback as she reviewed and edited each story. Most of all, she is one of the most caring people and brings out the best in everyone she meets. Thank you, Jennifer!

We met on the bus thirty-plus years ago, on the way to Washington D.C. Kara Rose and I were working on our master's degrees and soon after ended up in the same school district teaching art education. Our rooms were side by side. We had fun getting to know one another and loved sharing our stories. She often encouraged me to write a book. I always enjoyed her creative art work and asked if she would do the illustrations for some of my stories. I feel very blessed having her in my life and told her she is like a sister. Thank you, Kara, for your lovely illustrations.

Thanks to those who read my manuscript and gave good feedback and encouragement: Ruth Ann Kulp, Bev Mullen, John and Amy Bravis, Meta and Mark Meckstroth, and Reverend Ernie Hawk. I'm deeply appreciative and indebted to all those who have blessed me on my journey. I could never have done this alone. Thank you to those I met in several different creative writing classes who listened to my stories and provided valuable critiques. My list could go on and on because so many inspired me along the way. I value all my friendships and their inspiration.

I thank the Divine for helping me to keep focused and reminding me of what is most important...Love, Acceptance, Forgiveness, Joy, and to Live in the Moment.